Malcolm Arnold
Catalogue of works

Compiled by Alan Poulton
with a foreword by Julian Lloyd-Webber

Malcolm Arnold Society

Malcolm Arnold: Catalogue of works

Compiled by Alan Poulton

Published by The Malcolm Arnold Society,
    172 Bridport Road, Poundbury, Dorchester DT1 3AH
    Tel: 01305 319661; e-mail: alan@malcolmarnoldsociety.co.uk

© 2021 Alan Poulton and The Malcolm Arnold Society. All rights reserved.

ISBN: 9798701911244

Cover photo: Malcolm Arnold at the time of receiving his knighthood, December 1992.
Photo: Eastern Counties Newspapers

Contents

Malcolm Arnold at home in Attleborough, June 1991. Photo: Eastern Counties Newspapers

Foreword

Britain has produced comparatively few composers of genius but Malcolm Arnold is certainly one of them. Yet he is also one of the most misunderstood, partly because of his extraordinarily prolific output, which is so vividly highlighted by this new and exhaustive catalogue of his works.

Arnold composed one hundred and thirty-two film scores, twenty concertos and nine symphonies amongst a wealth of other music. His music is therefore hard to pigeon-hole, which is an inconvenience in a world that looks for quick, convenient answers.

Yet for those who are happy to listen to Arnold's music with an open mind there is an abundance of musical joy just waiting to be discovered within the opus numbers of this fascinating and greatly underrated composer.

So, amidst this plethora of riches, where to start? Perhaps the slow movement of the Second Symphony and all of the Fifth Symphony. On a smaller scale there is the Guitar Concerto, on a still smaller scale the Little Suites for Brass Band and, for a single instrument, the Fantasy for Cello which I will always be proud that he dedicated to me.

As Malcolm once said to me, "My music is a gesture of friendship," and his own music will continue to win him friends for time immemorial.

Julian Lloyd Webber

The Malcolm Arnold Society

promoting the music of one of Britain's greatest composers

Patrons John Gibbons, Keith Lockhart, Julian Lloyd Webber, John Wilson, Barry Wordsworth

For more details, please visit the web site: **www.malcolmarnoldsociety.co.uk**

Introduction

This latest catalogue of the music of Sir Malcolm Arnold is, in fact, the second revision of my original catalogue published by Faber in 1986. The first of these revisions was undertaken in 1999 as part of my three volume 'Dictionary of Modern British Composers', published by Greenwood Press (Connecticut, USA) in 2000.

Since then, there has been much increased activity both on the publications front and in the concert hall. This is reflected in the size and scope of this catalogue of works which the Malcolm Arnold Society are pleased to publish in this, Sir Malcolm Arnold's centenary year.

Third time around, I have attempted to include as much information on first performances around the world as possible, but one is limited by the lack of historical information available, particularly from each of Arnold's three major publishers. There may therefore be earlier first performances of which I am unaware, and the reader is urged to correct any errors of documentation or add missing information by contacting me through the Malcolm Arnold Society web site.

This catalogue lists separately ballets which have been based on Arnold's music (Appendix A), arrangements of Arnold's film music for the concert hall (Appendix B), Arnold's music for feature films and documentaries (Appendices C and D), and arrangements Arnold made of music by other composers (Appendix E).

Appendix F gives a list of many of the articles published in *Beckus* and *Maestro* over the last 30 years.

Recordings have been excluded, as Terry Cushion has already updated his comprehensive Discography; His latest edition is included as a Supplement to *Maestro* No.7 (October 2020).

My thanks to David Dunstan, editor of *Beckus*, the Society's quarterly newsletter, and my co-editor of *Maestro*, our annual journal, for his diligence and expertise in compiling the very useful indexes.

Alan Poulton
Poundbury, West Dorset
January 2021

References

'Beckus' refers to the quarterly newsletter of the Malcolm Arnold Society; see
    www.malcolmarnoldsociety.co.uk
'Maestro' refers to the annual journal of the Malcolm Arnold Society; see
    www.malcolmarnoldsociety.co.uk
'Rogue Genius' refers to Meredith, Anthony and Harris, Paul: 'Malcolm Arnold: Rogue
    Genius', Thames/Elkin, 2004

Catalogue of works

Haile Selassie: March for piano solo (1936)
The manuscript was sent to Boosey & Hawkes but returned by them on 8 September 1936 with the standard rejection note. The score is lost.

Two Canons for piano solo (c.1937)
[1. in E minor 2. in D major]
Notes Probably dating from 1937, these were compositional exercises for Philip Pfaff's classes.

Allegro for trumpet and piano (c.1937)
Notes Probably dating from 1937 and his lessons with Philip Pfaff.

Theme and Three Variations (Trumpeter) for piano solo (1937)
[Theme, Var.I (Fugato), Var.II (Bourree), Var.III (Marcia Funebre)]
First performance Mark Bebbington – Purcell Room, London, September 1991

Allegro in E minor for piano solo (1937)
Duration 40"
Publisher Queen's Temple Publications [QTP]

Three Piano Pieces (1937)
[1. Prelude 2. Air 3. Gigue]
Duration 3'30"
Publisher QTP

Serenade in G for piano solo (1937)
Duration 2'15"
Publisher QTP

The Fighting Temeraire: song for voice and piano (c.1937)
[Words: Sir Henry Newbolt]
Notes The story of the fighting ship Temeraire immortalised in the 1839 painting by JMW
    Turner
Article Richard Shaw, 'Investigating Sir Malcolm's Songs and Arias' – Beckus 48, Spring 2003. The score is lost.

[The] Dream City for piano (1938)
Duration 2'

First performance University of Texas, San Antonio, USA, March 2003
First UK performance Christopher Lee Guild/Clíodna Shanahan   Royal & Derngate,
    Northampton, 21 October 2006 (First Malcolm Arnold Festival)
Publisher QTP

(a) arranged for wind quintet by Paul Harris (2001)
Instrumentation Fl. Ob. Cl. Bsn. Hn.
Publisher QTP, 2001

(b) arranged for organ
First performance Jonathan Clarke – St Matthew's Church, Northampton, 18 October 2008
    (Third Malcolm Arnold Festival)

Beauty Haunts the Woods: song for voice and piano (1938)
[Words: Ruth Arnold]
Duration 2'
First public performance Claire Thompson (Sop.)/Scott Mitchell (Pno.) – Royal & Derngate,
    Northampton, 15 October 2017 (Twelfth Malcolm Arnold Festival)

(a) arranged for clarinet, voice and piano by Paul Harris (2006)
First performance Jessica Gillingwater (Sop.)/Jonathan Howse (Cl.)/Shuang Wang (Pno.) –
    Royal & Derngate, Northampton, 21 October 2006 (First Malcolm Arnold Festival)
Publisher QTP

Kensington Gardens: song cycle for medium voice and piano (1938)
[Words: Humbert Wolfe – 1. Night 2. Tulip 3. Noon 4. Daffodil 5. Lupin 6. Hawthorn Tree
    7. The Rose 8. Laburnum 9. The Chestnut and the Beech Tree]
Duration 7'30"
First performance (five songs) Ian Partridge (Ten.)/Richard Shaw (Pno.) – Wigmore Hall,
    London, 23 October 2001 (80th Birthday Concert)
First performance (four songs) Abigail Taylor (Sop.)/Alice Pinto (Pno.) – Royal & Derngate,
    Northampton, 15 October 2016 (Eleventh Malcolm Arnold Festival)
First performance (complete) Claire Thompson (Sop.)/Scott Mitchell (Pno.) – Royal &
    Derngate, Northampton, 15 October 2017 (Twelfth Malcolm Arnold Festival)
Publisher Novello (five songs) in 'Malcolm Arnold: Songs and Arias'; QTP (complete)
Article Gordon Pullin, 'Kensington Gardens' – Beckus 109, Summer 2018

Violin Sonata (1938)
Notes this elusive work, written in the summer of 1938, was mentioned by Malcolm in a BBC
Norfolk interview in 1991. The score is lost ['Rogue Genius'].

Day Dreams for piano (1938)
Duration 3'30"
Publisher QTP

Two Part Songs (1939)
[Words: Ernest Dowson 1. Spleen 2. Vitae Summa Brevis Spem Nos Uetat Incohare
    Longam*]
Duration 1'45"

First modern performance Festival Singers/Bernard West – St Matthew's Church, Northampton, 18 October 2008 (Third Malcolm Arnold Festival)
Publisher QTP
Notes* Translated as 'Experience of life teaches us not to entertain hopes for the future that are over-long.' [Horace, Odes I:4]

Rhapsody for solo piano (1939)
Notes Written in the summer of 1939 as a present for his mother. The score is lost.

Grand Fantasia for flute, trumpet and piano (c.1940)
First performance probably Richard Adeney (Fl.)/Malcolm Arnold (Tpt.)/Betty [Mills] Coleman (Pno.) – St Buryan, Cornwall, Summer 1940
First modern performance Sebastian Bell (Fl.)/John Wallace (Tpt.)/Richard Shaw (Pno.) – Wigmore Hall, London, 25 October 2001 (80th Birthday Concert)
First US performance Jupiter Symphony Chamber Players – Good Shepherd-Faith Presbyterian Church, New York City, 8 January 2018
Notes The piece is inscribed as 'Opus 973', 'composed by A. Youngman' and probably featured 'in Malcolm's series of Northampton concerts in 1941' ['Rogue Genius']
Publisher QTP (version for flute, clarinet and piano)

[as a ballet] Grand Fantasia Op 973: Ballet (2015)
Choreographer: Cecilia Macfarlane
First performance Oxford Youth Dance, with Jennifer Dyson (Fl)/Caroline Waddington (Cl.)/ Silvia Lucas (Pno.) – Royal & Derngate, Northampton, 17 October 2015 (Tenth Malcolm Arnold Festival)

Suite Bourgeoise: miniature trio for flute, oboe and piano (1940)
[1. Prelude 2. Tango (Elaine): Andante con moto 3. Dance: (Censored!) 4. Ballad: the introduction is marked 'Quasi Wurlitzer' 5. Valse (subtitled 'UGO' – a reference to the movement's dedicatee, Hugo Rignold)]
Dedication "for [crossed out]" but probably reads "Richard (Adeney) and Betty (Mills)"
Duration 13'
First performance Richard Adeney (Fl.)/Ivor Slaney (Ob.)/Malcolm Arnold (Pno.) – Royal College of Music, London, 1940
First US performance Iowa Wind Quintet – University of Iowa School of Music, 10 March 1995
First modern UK performance (omitting No.5) Simon Desorgher (Fl.)/Paul Goodey (Ob.)/Sally Mays (Pno.) – Avenue House, Finchley, North London, 2 February 1997
First modern performance (complete) Lucy Adams (Fl.)/Graeme Adams (Ob.)/Alan MacLean (Pno.) – Princess Hall, Cheltenham Ladies' College, 7 September 2001
First London performance (No.5 only) Sebastian Bell (Fl.)/Nicholas Daniel (Ob.)/Richard Shaw (Pno.) – Wigmore Hall, London, 25 October 2001 (80th Birthday Concert)
Publisher Emerson Edition; QTP
Articles (i) *Piers Burton-Page, 'An Arnold Premiere – Almost!' – *Beckus* 24, Spring 1997; *Maestro* 1, October 2014
(ii) Claire Dunham, 'Suite Bourgeoise rediscovered' – *Beckus* 57, Summer 2005; *Maestro* 6, October 2019
(iii) Intriplicate, 'Suite Success' – *Beckus* 58, Autumn 2005;

[as a ballet] Suite Bourgeoise: Ballet (2014)
Choreographer: Jo Meredith
First performance National Youth Ballet/Berkeley Ensemble – Stag Theatre, Sevenoaks,
    Kent, 11 August 2014 (three performances)
First London performance above artists – New Theatre, Wimbledon, 1 September 2014
Article Tony Meredith, 'A new Arnold dance work: Suite Bourgeoise' – Beckus 95, Winter
    2014

Sonata in G minor for flute and piano (1940)
Written for Richard Adeney
First performance Richard Adeney (Fl.)/Malcolm Arnold (Pno.) – Carnegie Library,
    Northampton, 29 March 1941
First London performance above artists – Royal College of Music, London, June 1941
    (Student Concert)
Notes In a letter dated 13th June 1995 Richard Adeney said that Arnold "wrote a flute
    sonata for me, signing it 'A. N. Other'. I'm sure that's lost". However, this piece may
    well have been an earlier version of the following work.

Sonata for flute and piano (1940 rev. 1942)
Written for Richard Adeney – the (revised) score is dated 12 November 1942
Duration 8'30"
First performance (1940 version) Richard Adeney (Fl.)/Malcolm Arnold (Pno.) –
    Northampton, 1940-41
First modern performance Richard Adeney (Fl.) with student pianist at the Royal Academy of
    Music, London, 13 October 1985
First modern concert performance Alex Jakeman (Fl.)/Sophie Warwick (Pno.) Royal &
    Derngate, Northampton, 18 October 2008 (Third Malcolm Arnold Festival)
Publisher QTP
Notes Richard Adeney recalls that "the original copy had the facetious title saying Sonate
    poor flute... (this) was an experiment in using strict 12-Tone serial technique and so, of
    course, it will sound very much unlike Malcolm Arnold!"

Pavane for flute and piano (1940)
Written for Richard Adeney
First performance Richard Adeney (Fl.)/Malcolm Arnold (Pno.) – Carnegie Library,
    Northampton, 1940
First London performance above artists – Royal College of Music, London, June 1941
    (Student Concert)
The score is lost.

Overture [Suite] for wind octet arranged by the composer for piano duet (1940)
Duration 4'
Instrumentation Fl. Cl. Bsn.(2) Tpt.(2) Tbn.(2)
Notes Only 31 bars were fully scored – the Overture has the same instrumentation as
    Stravinsky's Octet, a work which Malcolm Arnold had taken part in during his studies at
    the Royal College of Music, conducted by his composition teacher, Gordon Jacob.

(a) arranged for string orchestra by Philip Wood (1993)
Unpublished

(b) arranged for wind quintet by Uwe Radok (2006)
Instrumentation Fl. Ob. Cl. Bsn. Hn.
Publisher QTP

Ragtime: for two pianos (1940)
Duration 4'
Publisher QTP

(a) arranged for piano duet by David Wordsworth
First performance David Wordsworth and Matthew Hough – Royal & Derngate,
    Northampton, 19 October 2014 (Ninth Malcolm Arnold Festival)

Trio for flute, trumpet and cello (c. 1940)
Written for Richard Adeney and his younger sister, Charlotte, to play
First private performance Richard Adeney (Fl.)/Malcolm Arnold (Tpt.)/Charlotte Adeney (Vc.)
    – Royal College of Music, London, c. 1940
Notes Adeney recalls it being "only a little rumba and I'm pretty sure it was thrown away
    after use". The easy cello part was to suit Adeney's younger sister and the trumpet
    played muted throughout. The score is lost.

Phantasy for String Quartet (1941)
Duration 12'
First performance Student Quartet (Alec Lindsay, Desmond Mitchell, Leonard Lopes-
    Salzedo, and Pamela Hind) – Royal College of Music, London, June 1941 (the score was
    written in five days and completed on 17 June 1941)
First modern performance Allegri String Quartet – Purcell Room, London, 21 March 1996
First Europe performance Zsuzsa Debre Quartet – Moyland Castle, Germany, 15 January 2006
Publisher QTP
Notes (i) The Presto section was later incorporated into the Wind Quintet Op.2 and
    other sections into a projected first symphony (distinct from Arnold's first published
    symphony); the score of the Phantasy has a number of markings in red pencil to
    indicate instrumentation (flute, clarinets, trumpets etc.)
(ii) Originally entitled 'Vita Abundans', this work won second prize in the W W Cobbett
    competition: the winner that year was Ruth Gipps for her piano quartet entitled
    'Brocade', and for whom Arnold would later compose his Variations for Orchestra
    Op.122.
Articles (i) David Angel, 'Sir Malcolm Arnold's String Quartets' – *Beckus* 54, Autumn 2004;
    Maestro 5, October 2018
(ii) Piers Burton-Page, 'The Arnold quartets revisited' (with music examples) – *Maestro* 5,
    October 2018

Two Sketches for oboe and piano (1941)
Duration 5'
First performance Graeme Adams (Ob.)/Alan MacLean (Pno.) – Princess Hall, Cheltenham
    Ladies' College, 7 September 2001

Publisher QTP

Two Piano Pieces (1941)

Duration 2'30"
Publisher QTP

Flute Sonata in C major (1942)

First performance Madeau Stewart (Fl.)/Margaret Murray (Pno.) – Royal College of Music,
London, 2 February 1942 (Student Concert)
The score is lost.

Piano Sonata in B minor (1942)

Duration 10'
First performance Richard Deering – British Music Information Centre, London, 15 May 1984
First broadcast performance Richard Deering – BBC World Service, 3 August 1984
Publisher Roberton, 1984

**(a) arranged for saxophone and string orchestra (at the suggestion of the composer) by
David Ellis (1994)**
First performance Gerard McChrystal/Milton Keynes City Orchestra/Hilary Davan Wetton –
Stantonbury Campus Theatre, Milton Keynes, 10 February 1996
Publisher Roberton/Good Music, as 'Concerto for saxophone (2005)' – also arranged for
saxophone and piano

(b) arranged for saxophone and wind band by Mamoru Nakata (2001)
First performance Tokyo Kosei Wind Orchestra – Tokyo, Japan, 4 December 2001
Publisher Roberton/Good Music

---

*In an early diary entry around 1944 Malcolm Arnold made a start on assigning Opus
numbers which differed somewhat from the later, definitive listings. They were as follows:*
    Op.1 – Flute Sonata No.1 (possibly the 1940 Sonata in G minor – see above)
    Op.2 – Divertimento for orchestra (re-assigned as Op.1)
    Op.3 – Flute Sonata No.2 (possibly the 1940 Sonata for flute and piano – 1942
        revised version, see above, or even the missing 1942 Flute Sonata in C major)
    Op.4 – Wind Quintet (Op.2)
    Op.5 – Three Piano Pieces (not included in the definitive list)
    Op.6 – Larch Trees (Op.3)
    Op.7 – Three Shanties (Op.4)
    Op.8 – Beckus the Dandipratt (Op.5)
    Op.9 – Trio for flute, viola and bassoon (Op.6)
    Op.10 – Quintet (Op.7)
    Op.11 – Horn Concerto (Op.11)
    Op.12 – Variations for piano (Op.9)
*Arnold later removed the Op.3 Flute Sonata No.2 from the list, shifted all the numbers
back one space, until he reached the Horn Concerto which became Op.12 and Variations
for piano Op.10. Two new entries were the Duo for flute and viola Op.11 (Op.10 in the
definitive list) and Two Songs Op.13 (Op.8).*

Divertimento No.1 for orchestra Op.1 (1942)
Duration 10'30"
Instrumentation 3/2/2/2 – 4/3/3/1 – timp. perc.(2) str.
First performance London Symphony Orchestra/Benjamin Frankel – Guildhall School of
　　Music & Drama, London, 29 May 1945 (CPNM Concert)
Autograph MS untraced
Notes Arnold sent the score of this Op.1 to Sir Henry Wood in January 1943 – his reply
　　thanked him for "the loan of your score 'Divertimento' ... I regret very much that I
　　cannot find a place for it in my programmes at present." (Paul Jackson, 'The Brilliant
　　and the Dark', Ashgate, 2003, p.19).

Wind Quintet Op.2 (1942)
Written for the London Philharmonic Wind Quintet
Duration 13'
Instrumentation Fl. Ob. Cl. Hn. Bsn.
First performance London Philharmonic Wind Quintet – Richard Adeney (Fl.)/Michael
　　Dobson (Ob.)/John Lucas (Cl.)/Charles Gregory (Hn.)/George Alexandra (Bsn.) – Lourdes
　　Hall, Harpenden, Herts, 20 March 1943
First London performance above artists – Trinity College of Music, London, 7 June 1943
　　(CPNM Concert*)
First broadcast performance above artists – BBC European Service, 9 August 1943 (from the
　　Bristol Overseas Service Studios)
First modern performance Wind Quintet – Hartwell House, Aylesbury, 6 November 2002
First US performance Mary Karen Clardy (Fl.)/Charles Veazey (Ob.)/James Gillespie (Cl.)/
　　Kathleen Reynolds (Bsn.) and William Scharnberg (Hn.) – Denton College, University of
　　North Texas, 3 March 2003
Publisher QTP
Notes (i) For many years the score was lost and only came to light in 2002 through the
　　estate of Stephen Waters, a member of the Dennis Brain Wind Quintet.
(ii) *The Quintet received a second London performance at a CPNM Concert given at the
　　Salle Erard in Great Marlborough Street on 20 May 1947
Articles (i) Paul Harris 'Lost and Found' – *Beckus* 48, Spring 2003; *Maestro* 4, October 2017
(ii) David Morris 'Sixty Years Tacet' – *Beckus* 52, Spring 2004; *Maestro* 5, October 2018

Serenade for flute and piano (1943)
First performance probably Richard Adeney (Fl.) and Malcolm Arnold (Pno.)
The score is lost.

Three Piano Pieces (1943)
[1. Prelude 2. Romance 3. Lament]
Duration 7'30"
First modern performance Yonty Solomon – Purcell Room, London, 11 April 1996
Publisher QTP

Larch Trees: Tone poem for orchestra Op.3 (1943)
Duration 11'15"
Instrumentation 2/2/2/2 – 4/0/0/0 – str.

First performance London Philharmonic Orchestra/Malcolm Arnold – Royal Albert Hall, London, 1 October 1943 (CPNM Concert)
First modern performance London Repertoire Orchestra/Ruth Gipps – Guildhall School of Music & Drama, London, 26 February 1984
First broadcast performance Northern Sinfonia/Christopher Seaman – Radio 3, 7 December 1984
Publisher Faber, 1985
Article Alan Poulton, in 'Malcolm Arnold and Ruth Gipps' – Beckus 100, Spring 2016

Three Shanties for Wind Quintet Op.4 (1943)
Written for the London Philharmonic Wind Quintet to play on their wartime tours
Duration 6'30"
Instrumentation Fl. Ob. Cl. Hn. Bsn
First performance London Philharmonic Wind Quintet – Filton Aerodrome, Bristol, August 1943 (lunchtime recital, sometime between 2 and 7 August)
First broadcast performance Marsyas Wind Quintet – Home Service, 24 March 1953
Publisher Paterson, 1952; Carl Fischer (New York), 1967
Notes The Quintet features the sea shanties 'What shall we do with the drunken sailor?', 'Johnny come down to Hilo' and 'Boney was a warrior' to humorous effect.

(a) arranged for brass quintet by Dennis Wick (2001)
Instrumentation Hn. Tpt.(2) Tbn. Tba.
First concert performance Royal College of Music Brass Quintet – Royal & Derngate, Northampton, 6 October 2007 (Second Malcolm Arnold Festival)
First Europe performance Members of the Tonhalle Orchestra – Kleiner Saal, Tonhalle, Zurich, Switzerland, 11 September 2016
Publisher Novello, 2001

(b) arranged for wind octet by Joao Pereira (2014)
Dedicated to the Portuguese Navy Band Wind Octet
Instrumentation Ob.(2), Cl.(2), Hn.(2), Bsn.(2)
First performance Portuguese Navy Band Wind Octet/Joao Pereira – Lisbon, Portugal
Publisher Novello, 2014
Article Alan Poulton, 'Three Shanties arranged for octet' – Beckus 109, Summer 2018

(c) arranged for wind band by Jeff Krauklis (1989)
Unpublished

(d) arranged for small orchestra by Philip Lane (2003)
Instrumentation 2/1/2/1 – 2/1/0/0 – perc.(2) hp. str.
First performance BBC Concert Orchestra/Barry Wordsworth – Royal Festival Hall, London, 2 March 2005 (and broadcast 'live' on Radio 3)
Publisher Novello, 2005 (as Op.4a)

Beckus the Dandipratt: Comedy Overture for orchestra Op.5 (1943)
Duration 8'30"
Instrumentation 2+picc./2/2/2 – 4/2 + cnt./3/1 – timp. perc. str.
First performance BBC Scottish Orchestra/Ian Whyte – BBC Third Programme, 29 November 1946 (repeated on the Home Service, 25 September 1948)

First concert performance London Philharmonic Orchestra/Eduard van Beinum – Royal Opera House, Covent Garden, London, 16 November 1947
First US performance University of Illinois Symphony Orchestra/Rafael Kubelik – University Auditorium, Illinois, 29 March 1952
Publisher Lengnick, 1948
Notes The completion of the score at Capel Garmon, the same location as that of the 1941 Two Sketches for oboe and piano leaves to some speculation that 'Beckus' is perhaps an earlier work than 1943 or was at least begun while on holiday in North Wales.

Trio for flute, viola and bassoon Op.6 (1943)
Written for members of the London Philharmonic Orchestra
Duration 12'30"
First performance Richard Adeney (Fl.)/Wrayburn Glasspool (Va.)/George Alexandra (Bsn.) – Fyvie Hall, London, 18 January 1944 (CPNM Recital)
First broadcast performance Geoffrey Gilbert (Fl.)/Frederick Riddle (Va.)/Tom Wightman (Bsn.) – Third Programme, 13 November 1948 (repeated on 14 September 1949 and 17 January 1950)
Publisher Paterson, 1954

Quintet Op.7 (1944)
Written for members of the London Philharmonic Orchestra
Duration 13'30"
Instrumentation Fl. Vn. Va. Hn. Bsn.
First performance Richard Adeney (Fl.)/Albert Chasey (Vn.)/Wrayburn Glasspool (Va.)/ Charles Gregory (Hn.)/George Alexandra (Bsn.) – London, 21 December 1944 (National Gallery Concert)
First broadcast performance Geoffrey Gilbert (Fl.)/Thomas Peatfield (Vn.)/Harry Danks (Va.)/ Douglas Moore (Hn.)/Richard Newton (Bsn.) – Third Programme, 28 March 1950

The composer later revised the work in 1959-60
Duration 7'30"
First performance Geoffrey Gilbert (Fl.)/Granville Jones (Vn.)/Frederick Riddle (Va.)/Alan Civil (Hn.)/Gwydion Brooke (Bsn.) – Maida Vale Studios, London, 8 March 1960 (BBC Invitation Concert)
First broadcast performance above artists – Third Programme, 8 December 1960
Publisher Paterson, 1960

Burlesque for horn and orchestra (1944)
Duration 6'
Instrumentation picc+ 2/2/2/2-0/0/0/0 – timp.str.
First performance Martin Owen/Royal Philharmonic Orchestra/Barry Wordsworth – Royal & Derngate, Northampton, 22 October 2006 (First Malcolm Arnold Festival)
Publisher Novello (edited for performance by Philip Lane)
Notes This movement is completely different from the Horn Concerto No.1 dating from the following year – the title 'Burlesque' was added by the publishers.
Article Alan Poulton, 'Burlesque' (programme note, 22 October 2006)

Two songs for voice and piano Op.8 (1944)

[1 Neglected: (Mai Chang translated Arthur Waley [or possibly Herbert Giles*]) 2. Morning Moon (Maurice Carpenter)]
Duration 5'
First performance Joyce Newton (M/s)/Mabel Lovering (Pno.) – Salle Erard, London, 25 February 1947 (CPNM Recital)
First modern performance Georgina Anne Colwell (Sop.)/Nigel Foster (Pno.) – St Mary's Church, Alverstoke, Hampshire, 2 March 1996
First London performance Ian Partridge (Ten.)/Richard Shaw (Pno.) – Wigmore Hall, London, 23 October 2001 (80th Birthday Concert)
First Europe performance Gesine van der Grinten (M/s)/Raphael Thöne (Pno.) – Moyland Castle, Germany, 15 January 2006 (Moyland Festival)
Publisher Novello in 'Malcolm Arnold: Songs and Arias'
Article *Richard Shaw in 'Investigating Sir Malcolm's Songs and Arias' – Beckus 48, Spring 2003

No.2 'Morning Moon' for solo piano (1944) arranged by the composer
Publisher Novello, in 'Malcolm Arnold: Songs and Arias'

Variations on a Ukrainian Folk Song, for piano Op.9 (1944)

Dedicated "For John Kuchmy", a Ukrainian violinist in the London Philharmonic Orchestra, at whose suggestion the variations were written – the theme was later transformed into the popular song 'Yes, my darling daughter'.
Duration 15'
First performance Edith Vogel – Salle Erard, London, 19 November 1946 (CPNM Recital)
First Canada performance John Kuchmy – Canadian Broadcasting Company, October 1948
First public performance John Kuchmy – Wigmore Hall, London, 12 January 1949
First UK broadcast performance Edna Iles – Home Service, 7 February 1958 (repeated on 19 November 1960)
First Asia performance Moritz Ernst – Goethe Institute, Jakarta, Indonesia, 24 November 2014
Publisher Lengnick, 1948
Article Alan Poulton, in 'John Kuchmy – a man of many parts' – Beckus 96, Spring 2015
Notes An early copy of the printed score was inscribed by the composer "To Johnny, with best wishes, Malcolm – 28 October 1948" around the time of the Canadian premiere.

(a) arranged for string orchestra by Roger Steptoe (1993)
Commissioned by Alfred Lengnick
First performance Budapest String Orchestra – St Andrew's Hall, Norwich, 13 October 1993 (Norfolk and Norwich Festival)
First London performance Milton Keynes Chamber Orchestra/Hilary Davan Wetton – St John's Smith Square, London, 11 April 1994
First US performance Milton Keynes Chamber Orchestra/Hilary Davan Wetton – Stockton State College, Hermona, New Jersey, 26 April 1994
Publisher Lengnick, 1993

Duo for flute and viola Op.10 (1945)
Written for Richard Adeney and Wrayburn Glasspool

Duration 13'
First performance John Francis (Fl.)/Bernard Davies (Va.) – Salle Frard, London, 3 December
1946 (CPNM Recital)
First modern London performance Nancy Ruffer (Fl.)/Sue Bicknell (Va.) – British Music
Information Centre, London, 25 February 1993
First US performance Mark Holloway (Fl.)/unnamed violist – Boston, Massachusetts, 1
December 2000
First modern Europe performance Gabriella Sinay (Fl.)/unnamed violist – Moyland Castle,
Germany, 15 January 2006
First modern UK performance Claire Fillhart (Fl.)/Sian Stuart (Va.) – Royal & Derngate,
Northampton, 18 October 2008 (Third Malcolm Arnold Festival)
Publisher Faber, 1985

Concerto No.1 for horn and orchestra Op.11 (1945)
Dedicated to Charles Gregory, the first horn of the London Philharmonic
Duration 22'
Instrumentation 2+picc./2/2/2 – 0/0/0/0 – timp. str.
First performance Charles Gregory/London Philharmonic Orchestra/Ernest Ansermet – Royal
Opera House, Covent Garden, London, 8 December 1946
First broadcast performance Dennis Brain/BBC Midland Light Orchestra/Gilbert Vinter –
Midland Home Service (from Birmingham), 18 May 1951
First Europe performance Frank Lloyd/Popular University Orchestra/Tobias van der Locht –
Philharmonic Hall, Witten, Germany, 23 November 2017
Publisher Lengnick, 1947 (2nd movement arranged for horn and piano by the composer);
Complete Music Ltd, 1992 (complete horn and piano reduction)
Articles (i) Alan Poulton, 'Arnold's first concerto performance' – Beckus 96, Spring 2015
(ii) William C. Lynch, in 'Brothers in Brass: the friendship of Malcolm Arnold and Dennis
Brain' (with music examples) – Maestro 2, October 2015

Symphonic Suite for orchestra Op.12 (1945)
Written in memory of the composer's brother, Philip, who was killed in the Second World
War
Duration 15'
Instrumentation 2 + picc./2/2/2 – 4/3/3/1 – timp. perc.(2) str.
Notes Material from the first movement was later incorporated into the Little Suite No.1
Op.53 q.v. The original score is lost.

Prelude for piano (1945)
Duration 2'45"
Publisher QTP

Symphony for string orchestra Op.13 (1946)
Written for the Riddick String Orchestra
Duration 22'
First performance Riddick String Orchestra/Kathleen Riddick – Kensington Town Hall,
London, 29 April 1947

Catalogue of works

First broadcast performance Jacques Orchestra/Reginald Jacques – Third Programme, 21 January 1948 (repeated on the Home Service, 6 April 1948 and the Third Programme, 7 July 1949)
First Russia performance Moscow21 Ensemble – Tchaikovsky Hall, Moscow, 20 June 1996
First Europe performance Essen Philharmonic Orchestra – Kevelaer Cathedral, Germany, 17 November 2001
First US performance Longy Chamber Orchestra/Janet Packer – Longy School of Music, Cambridge, Massachusetts, April 2006
Publisher Lengnick, 1946
Notes Arnold's first wife, Sheila Nicholson, played violin in the Riddick String Orchestra
Article Günther Kögebehn 'Symphony for strings' concert review – Beckus 112, Spring 2019

Festival Overture for orchestra Op.14 (1946)
Written for Philip Pfaff* and the Ipswich Orchestral Society
Duration 6'
Instrumentation 2/2/2/2 – 2/2/0/0 – timp. str.
First performance Ipswich Orchestral Society/Philip Pfaff – Ipswich Public Hall, 12 March 1947
First London performance East Ham Symphony Orchestra/Philip Pfaff – East Ham, 16 February 1952
Notes (i) *Philip Pfaff, a former organist of St Matthew's Church in Northampton, had taught Arnold in the early thirties. (See also Laudate Dominum Op.25)
(ii) There was a further performance of the Overture, also conducted by Pfaff, by the Trent Park College Orchestra in the 1960s – thereafter the score was lost. There was a possibility of a performance nearly three decades later when the English Sinfonia conducted by Philip's son, Graham, were slated to perform the Overture at the Royal & Derngate, Northampton on 12 September 1987. The hoped-for score clearly never emerged from hiding.
Article Alan Poulton, 'The Ipswich Festival Overture' – Beckus 94, Autumn 2014

Sonata No.1 for violin and piano Op.15 (1947)
Duration 15'
First performance Nona Liddell (Vn.)/Daphne Ibbott (Pno.) – Arts Council Drawing Room, London, 2 October 1951 (CPNM Recital)
First broadcast performance above artists – Radio 3, 19 April 1985
First Europe performance Gerd Jansen – Germany, 11 June 2005
Publisher Lengnick, 1947

Children's Suite for piano Op.16 (1947)
[I. Prelude (Study in Fourths and Fifths), II. Carol (Study in Legato Thirds for Left Hand), III. Shepherd's Lament (Study in Triplets and Accidentals), IV. Trumpet Tune (Study in Trills and Rhythmic Playing), V. Blue Tune (Study in Rhythms and Colour), VI. Folk Song (Study in Touch and Phrasing)]
Duration 5'
Publisher Lengnick, 1948

(a) arranged for recorder quartet by Denis Bloodworth
First performance Society of Recorder Players – Norfolk, 18 November 1995 (and in the presence of the composer)

13

Publisher Lengnick/Complete Music, 1993 (as 'Miniature Suite Op.16a')
Article Denis Bloodworth, in 'Sir Malcolm Arnold and the recorder' – *Beckus* 21, Summer
  1996, Maestro 1, October 2014

Sonata for viola and piano Op.17 (1947)
Dedicated to Frederick Riddle
Duration 13'
First performance Frederick Riddle (Va.)/Frederick Stone (Pno.) – BBC Latin American
  Service, 1948
First UK broadcast performance Watson Forbes (Va.)/Alan Richardson (Pno.) – Third
  Programme, 22 November 1949
Publisher Lengnick, 1948

Two Bagatelles for piano Op.18 (1947)
Duration 4'45"
First performance Richard Deering – British Music Information Centre, London, 15 May 1984
First Europe performance Antonio Piricone – Saal der Musikschule, Neu-Ulm, Germany, 11
  May 2001
Publisher Paterson, 1988

Sonatina for flute and piano Op.19 (1948)
Dedicated to Richard Adeney
Duration 8'
First performance Richard Adeney (Fl.)/Ernest Lush (Pno.) – c.1948
First broadcast performance (regional) Gareth Morris (Fl.)/Leo Wurmser (Pno.) – Midland
  Home Service (from Birmingham), 14 May 1951 (The Monday Concert – 'Three
  Northamptonshire composers')
First broadcast performance (national) Richard Adeney (Fl.)/Frederick Stone (Pno.) – Third
  Programme, 20 October 1952
Publisher Lengnick, 1948

(a) arranged for flute and string orchestra by David Ellis (2000)
First performance Esther Ingham/Northern Chamber Orchestra/Nicholas Ward –
  Macclesfield, Cheshire, Autumn 2001 (70th birthday concert)
First Europe performance Camerata Gothia – Moindal, Sweden, 1 March 2011
First US performance CSU Philharmonic Orchestra – Columbia State University, Columbus,
  Georgia, 4 March 2015
Publisher Lengnick/Complete Music Ltd, as 'Concertino for flute and strings Op.19a (2000)'

(b) Excerpt 'Blues' (third movement) arranged for flute and string orchestra by
  Christopher Palmer
Unpublished

Music for a Pageant: composite work (1948)
[Scenario: Montagu Slater]
Written to mark the centenary of the Communist Manifesto – Arnold's contribution was
a 'Factory Scene' in two parts. Among the other composers were Christian Darnton and
Bernard Stevens.

Duration 10-12' (Factory scene)
First performance Birmingham Clarion Singers/London Communist Choir/augmented Wind
Band/Alan Bush – Royal Albert Hall, London, 30 March 1948
Article Alan Poulton, 'Arnold and a Communist Pageant' (with music examples) – *Beckus*
119, Winter 2020

To Youth: Suite for orchestra (1948)
[I. Prelude II. Pastoral III. March: Allegro con brio]
Written for Ruth Railton and the National Youth Orchestra of Great Britain for their
inaugural concert
Duration 9'30"
Instrumentation 2/2/2/2 – 4/3/3/1 – timp. perc.(2) str.
First performance National Youth Orchestra of Great Britain/Reginald Jacques – The
Pavilion, Bath, 21 April 1948
First broadcast performance above artists – BBC Home Service (Scottish) 11 June 1954 (a
recording of the premiere)
Publisher Paterson, 1956 (as Little Suite No.1 Op.53 q.v.)
Notes the first broadcast announced the work as 'Salute for Youth'.

Concerto No.1 for clarinet and string orchestra Op.20 (1948)
Dedicated to Frederick Thurston
Duration 16'30"
First performance Frederick Thurston/Jacques Orchestra/Reginald Jacques – Freemasons'
Hall, Edinburgh, 29 August 1949 (Edinburgh International Festival)
First broadcast performance above artists – Light Programme, 20 September 1949 (Concert
Hour)
First Europe performance above artists – Hamburg, 20 February 1950 (on a European tour
which included Düsseldorf and Berlin)
First London performance above artists – South Kensington, 8 July 1950 (Museum Gardens
Concert)
First US performance Benny Goodman/California Chamber Symphony Orchestra/Hendi
Temianka – Royce Hall, University of California, Los Angeles, 2 October 1967
First Russia performance Moscow21 Ensemble – Tchaikovsky Hall, Moscow, 20 June 1996
Publisher Lengnick, 1952 (also arranged for clarinet and piano)
Articles (i) Janet Hilton, 'Playing Malcolm's clarinet works' – *Beckus* 101, Summer 2016
(ii) Alan Poulton, 'Clarinet concerto and sonatina' – *Beckus* 105, Summer 2017
(iii) Isaac Adni, 'Malcolm Arnold's concertos: masterpieces of mélange' (with music
examples) – *Maestro* 5, October 2018

The Smoke: Overture for orchestra Op.21 (1948)
Dedicated to Rudolf Schwarz and the Bournemouth Municipal Orchestra
Duration 7'
Instrumentation 2+picc./2/2/2 – 4/3/3/1 – timp. perc.(3) hp. str.
First performance Bournemouth Municipal Orchestra/Rudolf Schwarz – Royal Albert Hall,
London, 24 October 1948
First broadcast performance BBC Northern Orchestra/Lawrence Leonard – General Overseas
Service, 7 July 1957

Publisher Lengnick, 1948
Notes 'The Smoke' is a Cockney term for London.

Symphony No.1 Op.22 (1949)
Written for the Cheltenham Festival
Duration 28'30"
Instrumentation 2 + picc/2/2/2 – 4/3/3/1 – timp. perc. hp. str.
First performance Hallé Orchestra/Malcolm Arnold – Cheltenham Town Hall, 6 July 1951
  (Cheltenham Festival)
First London performance London Philharmonic Orchestra/Malcolm Arnold – Royal Festival
  Hall, London, 16 November 1951
First broadcast performance (regional) BBC Northern Orchestra/John Hopkins – Northern
  Home Service (from Manchester) 16 January 1953
First broadcast performance (national) above performance – Third Programme, 1 April 1953
First US performance Susquehanna Symphony Orchestra/Sheldon Bair – John Carroll School,
  Bel Air, Maryland, 20 October 2001 (Silver Anniversary season – at a concert celebrating
  the composer's 80th birthday)
Publisher Lengnick, 1952

Fanfare for three trumpets (1949)
Written for a civic reception on behalf of the Northampton Arts Association
First performance members of the Northampton Symphony Orchestra brass section/
  R Richardson-Jones – Northampton Town Hall, 21 October 1949 (Malcolm's 28th
  birthday).
The score is lost.

String Quartet No.1 Op.23 (1949)
Duration 18'45"
First performance New London String Quartet – BBC Third Programme, 13 November 1950
First concert performance New London String Quartet – Institute of Contemporary Arts,
  London, 26 October 1951
Publisher Lengnick, 1951
Articles (i) David Angel, 'Sir Malcolm Arnold's String Quartets' – *Beckus* 54, Autumn 2004;
  Maestro 5, October 2018
(ii) Piers Burton-Page, 'The Arnold Quartets revisited' (with music examples) – *Maestro* 5,
  October 2018

Henri Christophe: unfinished Opera in four Acts (1949)
[Libretto: Joe Mendoza]
Commissioned by the Arts Council of Great Britain for the Festival of Britain
Characters: Brelle (Ten.), Vastey (Bar.), Phoebe (M/s), Henri (Bs.)
Setting: The northern coast of Haiti, the western half of the island of San Domingo in the
  Caribbean – the year 1811
Duration projected 3 hours
Instrumentation 3/2/2/2 – 4/3/3/1 – timp. perc.(2) hp. str. (+ four soloists)
First performance (Overture and the incomplete first scene which includes Phoebe's song)

soloists of Nevill Holt Opera/The Ely Sinfonia/Steve Bingham – Royal & Derngate, Northampton, 15 October 2016 (Eleventh Malcolm Arnold Festival)

Notes Henri Christophe was a general who became the first black ruler of Haiti. He shot himself with a golden bullet when there was a popular uprising against him. The opera was intended for performance at the Festival of Britain in 1951 but was turned down on submission of the draft. Arnold only completed 205 bars (27 pages) of full score: this included an Overture leading directly into Act I Scene I.

Articles (i) Joe Mendoza, 'Me and Malcolm Arnold' – *Beckus* 37, Summer 2000 & *Maestro* 1, October 2014

(ii) Lewis Foreman, 'Henry Christophe: killed by bureaucracy', with music examples and Appendices – *Maestro* 2, October 2015

(ii) Alan Poulton, 'Up at the Villa' – *Beckus* 101, Summer 2016

Divertimento No.2 for orchestra Op.24 (1950)

[I. Fanfare II. Nocturne III. Chaconne]
Written for the National Youth Orchestra of Great Britain for their first European tour
Duration 9'
Instrumentation 2+picc./2/2/2 – 4/3/3/1 – timp. perc.(2) hp. str.
First performance National Youth Orchestra of Great Britain/Malcolm Arnold – The Dome, Brighton, 19 April 1950
First Europe performance above artists – Palais de Chaillot, Paris, 21 April 1950 (and repeated in the Salle Pleyel, Paris, on 22 April)
First broadcast performance above artists – Third Programme, 28 August 1950
First Scotland performance National Youth Orchestra of Great Britain/Walter Susskind – Usher Hall, Edinburgh, 2 September 1951(Edinburgh International Festival)
First London performance National Youth Orchestra of Great Britain/Hugo Rignold – Royal Albert Hall, London, 10 August 1957 (Promenade Concert)
Publisher Paterson, 1961 (as Op.75 q.v.)
Article Alan Poulton, 'The National Youth Orchestra and Malcolm Arnold – and the mystery of Divertimento No.2' (with music examples) – *Maestro* 2, October 2015

Fantasy for bass trombone and piano (1950)

Written for Mike Payne (a member of the National Youth Orchestra of Great Britain) to use as an audition piece
Duration 3'
Article Stan Hibbert in the *Gramophone*'s 75th Birthday tribute, October 1996.
The score is lost.

Psalm 150 'Laudate Dominum' for SATB chorus and organ Op.25 (1950)

Commissioned by and dedicated "For the Rev Canon Walter Hussey, the Choir and Organist of St Matthew's Church, Northampton"
Duration 7'
First performance St Matthew's Church Choir, with Philip Pfaff (organ) – St Matthew's Church, Northampton, 21 September 1950
First broadcast performance BBC Chorus/Leslie Woodgate, with Charles Spinks (organ) – Third Programme, 26 June 1952 (and repeated on the Home Service, 21 June 1954)

First documented London performance Royal Academy of Music Chamber Choir –
Marylebone Parish Church, London, 20 June 1996 (British and American Film Music
Festival)
Publisher Lengnick, 1950

Serenade for small orchestra Op.26 (1950)
Written for the Hampton Court Serenade Concerts
Duration 13'30"
Instrumentation 2/2/2/2 – 2/2/0/0 – timp. str.
First performance New London Orchestra/Alec Sherman – The Orangery, Hampton Court, 4
June 1950 (Serenade Concert)
First broadcast performance Kalmar Chamber Orchestra/Colin Davis – Home Service, 30
March 1955
Publisher Lengnick, 1950

[as a ballet] MA Serenade: Ballet (2014)
Choreographer: Ronn Tice
First performance Whilbey Island Dance Theatre – Langley, Washington, August 2014
Article Alan Poulton, 'Arnold's other ballets' – *Maestro* 4, October 2017

English Dances for orchestra (Set 1) Op.27 (1950)
Dedicated "For Bernard de Nevers"*
Duration 8'
Instrumentation 2+picc./2/2/2 – 4/3/3/1 – timp. perc.(2) cel. hp. str.
First performance London Philharmonic Orchestra/Sir Adrian Boult – Central Hall, East Ham,
London, 14 April 1951
First broadcast performance BBC Northern Orchestra/Charles Groves – Home Service, 15
September 1951 (repeated on the Third Programme, 20 November 1951 and on the Light
Programme, 18 December 1951)
Publisher Lengnick, 1951
Notes (i) *Arnold's publisher, whose idea it was to produce a set equal in popularity to
the Dvořák Slavonic Dances. This and the second set of English Dances were later
incorporated in to the Ballet 'Solitaire' q.v.
(ii) Dance No.4 was used for the BBC Television series 'Get Ahead', presented by Peter
West, the final of which was relayed from the Carlton Rooms, Maida Vale, on 24 May
1962.

(a) arranged for piano duet by Franz Reizenstein (1958)
First modern performance David Wordsworth and Matthew Hough – Royal & Derngate,
Northampton, 19 October 2014 (Ninth Malcolm Arnold Festival)
Publisher Lengnick, 1958

(b) arranged for wind band by Maurice Johnstone (1965)
Publisher Lengnick, 1965

(c) arranged for military band (c.1989)
First UK performance RAF Central Band/Wing Cdr Barrie Hingley – Royal Northern College of
Music, Manchester, 3 November 1989 (BASWBE Concert)

(d) arranged for brass band by Ray Farr (1985)
First performance Grimethorpe Colliery Band/Elgar Howarth – 1 February 1993
First London performance Grimethorpe Colliery Band/Elgar Howarth – Queen Elizabeth Hall,
    London, 27 September 2004
Publisher Lengnick, 1993; Hal Leonard, 2019

**(e) Nos. 1 and 3 arranged by Paul Harris for flute or clarinet (or oboe or violin) and piano
    (2004)**
Publisher Lengnick, 2004

(f) Selection of dances arranged for recorder ensemble by Denis Bloodworth
Unpublished

Sonatina for oboe and piano Op.28 (1951)
Written for Léon Goossens
Duration 7'30"
First performance Léon Goossens (Ob.)/John Wilson (Pno.) – Northern School of Music,
    Manchester, 15 January 1952
First London performance Léon Goossens (Ob.)/Mabel Lovering (Pno.) – Croydon Civic Hall,
    October 1952
First broadcast performance Peter Graeme (Ob.)/Josephine Lee (Pno.) – Home Service, 10
    April 1953
Publisher Lengnick, 1951

(a) arranged for oboe and string orchestra by Roger Steptoe (1992)
First performance Nicholas Daniel/City of London Sinfonia/Christopher Robinson –
    Bromsgrove, Worcestershire, 7 May 1994 (Bromsgrove Festival)
First US performance Pro Arte Chamber Orchestra of Boston – Delray Beach, Florida, 8
    November 1998
Publisher Lengnick, 1994 (as 'Concertino for oboe and strings Op.28a')

Up at the Villa: unfinished Opera in one act (1951)
[Libretto: Joe Mendoza after Robert Browning]
Notes Preliminary sketches only – later discarded
Article Alan Poulton, 'Up at the Villa' – *Beckus* 101, Summer 2016

Sonatina for clarinet and piano Op.29 (1951)
Written for Frederick Thurston
Duration 7'45"
First performance Colin Davis (Cl.)/Geoffrey Corbett (Pno.) – Gallery of the Royal Society of
    British Architects, London, 20 March 1951
First broadcast performance Cyril Chapman (Cl.)/Tom Bromley (Pno.) – Midland Home
    Service (from Birmingham), 15 June 1954
First Asia performance Urs Brugger (Cl.)/Moritz Ernst (Pno.) – Goethe Institute, Jakarta,
    Indonesia, 24 November 2014
Publisher Lengnick, 1951
Notes According to Colin Bradbury the first private performance of the work was given by
    Frederick Thurston and Thea King in Hull during the New Year course with the National
    Youth Orchestra of Great Britain in January 1951

Article Alan Poulton, in 'Clarinet concerto and sonatina' – *Beckus* 105, Summer 2017

(a) arranged for clarinet and string orchestra by Roger Steptoe (1990)
First performance Angela Malsbury/Primavera Ensemble/Paul Manley – Newbury, Berkshire, 14 May 1991 (Newbury Festival)
First US performance Arapahoe Philharmonic Orchestra – Englewood, California, 5 February 1999
Publisher Lengnick, as 'Concertino for clarinet and strings Op.29a (1993)'
Article Alan Poulton, 'Works for soloists and strings' – *Beckus* 101, Summer 2016

(b) arranged for clarinet and wind band by Rodney Parker (2000)
Publisher Lengnick

(c) arranged for clarinet and accordion
First performance Magnus Holmander (Cl.)/Irina Serotyuk (Acc.) – Allhelgonakyrkan, Stockholm, Sweden, 6 April 2019

Symphonic Study ('Machines') for brass, percussion and strings Op.30
Duration 6'
Instrumentation 0/0/0/0 – 4/3/3/1 – timp. perc.(2) str.
First performance BBC Scottish Symphony Orchestra/Sir Charles Groves – Henry Wood Hall, Glasgow, 5 October 1984
First broadcast performance above performance – Radio 3, 16 October 1984
First London performance BBC Concert Orchestra/Carl Davis – BBC Maida Vale Studios, London, 18 October 1994
Publisher Faber, 1984
Notes A re-working of the documentary film music 'Report on Steel'

A Sussex Overture for orchestra Op.31 (1951)
Commissioned by the Festival of Brighton and dedicated "Herbert Menges and the Brighton Philharmonic Society" [later known as the Southern Philharmonic Orchestra]
Duration 8'30"
Instrumentation 2+picc/2/2/2 – 4/3/3/1 – timp. perc.(2) str.
First performance Southern Philharmonic Orchestra/Herbert Menges – The Dome, Brighton, 29 July 1951
First broadcast performance BBC Northern Orchestra/Lawrence Leonard – Light Programme, 8 August 1957 (repeated on the Home Service, 20 December 1957)
Publisher Lengnick, 1951
Notes The composer comments that "the music is an attempt to express the feeling of exhilaration that comes over one when walking on the downs or by the sea in Sussex". The work was revived at the 1985 Brighton Festival.

Concerto for piano duet and string orchestra Op.32 (1951)
Written at the suggestion of Mosco Carner and dedicated to Helen Pyke (Dr Carner's wife) and Paul Hamburger.
Duration 21'30"
First performance Helen Pyke/Paul Hamburger/Goldsbrough Orchestra/Mosco Carner – BBC Third Programme, 17 August 1951 (repeated on 9 November 1952 and on the Home Service, 15 November 1952)

First concert performance Helen Pyke/Paul Hamburger/Bournemouth Municipal Orchestra/ Charles Groves – Winter Gardens, Bournemouth, June 1953
First London performance Helen Pyke/Paul Hamburger/London Symphony Orchestra/Basil Cameron – Royal Albert Hall, London, 31 July 1953 (Promenade Concert)
First US performance Georgia and Louise Mangos – Norris Arts Centre, St Charles, Illinois, 28 July 2001
Publisher Lengnick, 1951 (piano score)

English Dances for orchestra (Set 2) Op.33 (1951)

Dedicated "For Bernard de Nevers", Arnold's publisher (see also Op.27)
Duration 9'
Instrumentation 3/2/2/2 – 4/3/3/1 – timp. perc. cel. hp. str.
First performance BBC Symphony Orchestra/Sir Malcolm Sargent – Royal Albert Hall, London, 5 August 1952 (Promenade Concert)
First broadcast performance BBC Scottish Orchestra/Alexander Gibson – Light Programme, 24 March 1953 (and repeated on the Home Service, 7 May 1953)
Publisher Lengnick, 1951
Notes (i) This and the first set of English Dances were later incorporated into the ballet Solitaire q.v.
(ii) Dance No.1 was famously used as the theme music to the Granada television series (later on Channel 4 and Radio 4 between 2010-2016) entitled 'What the Papers Say'. The same dance was also used in three episodes of the BBC Television series 'Spitting Image' between April 1984 and February 1985.

(a) arranged for piano duet by Franz Reizenstein (1958)

First modern performance David Wordsworth and Matthew Hough – Royal & Derngate, Northampton, 19 October 2014 (Ninth Malcolm Arnold Festival)
Publisher Lengnick, 1958

(b) arranged for wind band* by Nigel Herbert (1980)

Publisher Lengnick
Notes *There is another (unpublished) wind band arrangement by James Sudduth (1995)

(c) arranged for brass band by Ray Farr (1985)

First performance Grimethorpe Colliery Band/Elgar Howarth – 1 February 1993
Firtst London performance Grimethorpe Colliery Band/Elgar Howarth – Queen Elizabeth Hall, London, 27 September 2004
Publisher Lengnick, 1993; Hal Leonard, 2019

(d) No.5 arranged for brass ensemble by Ken Ferguson and Timothy Carding-Allen (no date)

Written for the English Brass Consort
Instrumentation Tpt.(4), Tbn.(4) Tba. timp. perc.
Unpublished

(e) Nos.5, 6 and 7 arranged for flute or clarinet (or oboe or violin) and piano by Paul Harris (2004)

Publisher Lengnick, 2004

(f) Selection of dances arranged for recorder ensemble by Denis Bloodworth
Unpublished

The Dancing Master: Opera in one Act Op.34 (1952)
[Libretto: Joe Mendoza based on a play by William Wycherley]
Score dated London, 18 May 1952
Duration 68'
Instrumentation 1+picc./2/2/2 – 4/3/3/1 – timp. perc (2). cel. hp. str.
First performance (piano version) cond. Lucy Reynolds – Barnes Music Club, Kitson Hall,
    Barnes, 1 March 1962 (as a double bill with Anthony Collins's *Catherine Parr*)
    Producer: Leigh Howard
    Choreography: Herald Braune
    Decor: Jane Pearson-Gee and David Kentish
    Principals: Guelda Cunningham, Margaret Lindsay, Donald Franke and Fergus O'Kelly.
First broadcast performance (with orchestra) BBC National Orchestra of Wales/James Holmes
    – Radio 3, 21 October 2006 (recorded at Broadcasting House, Cardiff, 25-26 May 2006).
    Principals: Ailish Tynan and Susan Gorton (Sops.); Wendy Dawn Thompson (M/s); Justin
    Lavender and Charles Daniels (Tens.) and Stephen Varcoe (Bar.)
First (semi-staged) performance (with orchestra) Ealing Symphony Orchestra/John Gibbons.
    Principals: Jessica Gillingwater (Miranda); Victoria Barton (Prue); William Davies
    (Monsieur); Stefan Berkieta (Don Diego); Stuart Overington (Gerard) and Lucilla
    Graham (Mrs Caution) – Royal & Derngate, Northampton, 20 October 2012 (Seventh
    Malcolm Arnold Festival)
First staged performance (with orchestra) Guildhall School of Music Orchestra/Dominic
    Wheeler – Silk Street Theatre, Barbican Centre, London, 2 March 2015 (and three further
    performances).
    Principals: Alison Rose (Miranda); Emma Kerr (Prue); Robin Bailey (Monsieur); David
    Shipley (Don Diego); Lawrence Thackeray (Gerard) and Ailsa Mainwaring (Mrs Caution)
Publisher Paterson/Novello; Novello (Excerpts in 'Malcolm Arnold: Songs and Arias' – 1.
    Gerard's first aria 2. Don Diego's aria)
Notes (i) There were plans to stage 'The Dancing Master' in London as early as the summer
    of 1987 with three performances at St Paul's Church, Hammersmith by Opera Viva
    conducted by Leslie Head (24, 25, and 26 June). Arnold's 80th birthday in 2001 brought
    an announcement that the opera would be staged at five venues including the Opera
    House in Buxton, the Theatre Royal in Margate and the English Music Festival in
    Stratford-upon-Avon.
Articles (i) Joe Mendoza, 'Malcolm Arnold and me' – *Beckus* 37, Summer 2000; *Maestro* 1,
    October 2014
(ii) Roger Heywood, 'The Dancing Master' – *Beckus* 68, Spring 2008
(iii) Paul Harris, 'The Dancing Master' – *Beckus* 85, Summer 2012
(iv) Lewis Foreman, 'The Dancing Master' – *Beckus* 97, Summer 2015
(v) Alan Poulton, 'Up at the Villa – Appendix 1' – *Beckus* 101, Summer 2016
(vi) Michael Jameson, 'New recording of The Dancing Master' – *Beckus* 119, Winter 2020

Two Ceremonial Psalms for unaccompanied SSA boys' chorus Op.35 (1952)
I.   O come, let us sing unto the Lord (Psalm 95)
II. Make a joyful noise unto the Lord (Psalm 100)

Written for Ann Mendoza, the sister of Joe Mendoza, librettist of The Dancing Master
Duration 5'
First performance Roehampton Choir – Marble Arch Synagogue, London, January 1952 (at Ann Mendoza's wedding to Philip Goldesgeyme)
First public performance (No.II only) Hastings Girls' Choir – White Rock Pavilion, Hastings, Sussex, 25 April 1954
First broadcast performance Dumbarton Ladies' Choir/George MacVicar – Scottish Home Service (from Glasgow), 28 February 1957 (repeated on the Midland Home Service, 30 July 1963)
First London public performance Royal Academy of Music Chamber Choir – Marylebone Parish Church, London, 20 June 1996 (British and American Film Music Festival)
Publisher Paterson, 1952
Article Alan Poulton, 'Up at the Villa', Appendix 2 – Beckus 101, Summer 2016

Eight Children's Piano Pieces Op.36 (1952)

[I. Tired Bagpipers II. Two Sad Hands III. Across the Plains IV. Strolling Tune V. Dancing Tune VI. Giants VII. The Duke goes a-hunting VIII. The Buccaneer]
Duration 9'45"
First broadcast performance (No.VIII only) Neil Wilson – Home Service, 17 December 1954 (recorded at the Wigmore Hall, London, during the National Junior Piano Competition prize-winners' concert)
First broadcast performance (excerpts) Sidney Harrison – Home Service, 8 February 1955
Publisher Lengnick, 1952 (in the series 'Five by Ten' ed. Alex Rowley); QTP

(a) Nos. IV to VIII (5 movements) arranged for recorder quartet by Denis Bloodworth (1993)
Duration 6'
Instrumentation Desc. Treb. Ten. Bs.
First performance Society of Recorder Players – Norfolk, 18 November 1995 (and in the presence of the composer)
Publisher Lengnick (as 'Miniature Suite')

(b) Nos. IV to VIII (5 movements) arranged for saxophone quartet by Denis Bloodworth (1992)
Instrumentation Sop. Al. Ten. Bs.
Publisher Lengnick, 1992

(c) arranged for orchestra as 'Children's Suite' Op.36a by Denis Bloodworth (1995)
Instrumentation 2/2/2/2 – 4/3/3/1 – timp. perc. str.
First performance Godalming Youth Orchestra/David Wright – Great Hall, Farnham Maltings, Surrey, 18 March 1997 (Farnham Festival)
Article Denis Bloodworth, 'Children's Suite' – Beckus 25, Summer 1997; Maestro 1, October 2014
Publisher Good Music, 1999

(d) Excerpt No.VIII 'The Buccaneer', arranged for orchestra by Tobias van der Locht (2003)
First performance Musica Art Orchestra of Sofia/Martin Panteleev – St Markus Church, Schneppenbaum, Germany, 15 June 2003
Unpublished

Divertimento for wind trio Op.37 (1952)
Duration 8'45"
Instrumentation Fl. Ob. Cl.
First performance Richard Adeney (Fl.), Sidney Sutcliffe (Ob.) and Stephen Waters (Cl.) –
    Mercury Theatre, Notting Hill Gate, London, 1953 (Macnaghten Concert)
First broadcast performance Members of the Virtuoso Chamber Ensemble – Third
    Programme, 12 November 1953 (repeated on 16 February 1954)
Publisher Paterson, 1952

The Sound Barrier: Rhapsody for orchestra Op.38 (1952)
Duration 7'30"
Instrumentation 2+picc/2/2/2 – 4/3/3/1 – timp. perc.(2) hp. cel. str.
First performance Liverpool Philharmonic Orchestra/Muir Mathieson – Anfield Stadium,
    Liverpool, 21 June 1952 (a concert of music from the films – Malcolm's score was only
    completed on 31 May)
First broadcast performance Ulster Orchestra/Yannis Daras – BBC Radio 3, 23 May 1984*
Publisher Paterson, 1952
Notes (i) Derived from the film of the same name
(ii) *Malcolm Arnold recorded the Rhapsody with the Royal Philharmonic Orchestra on 24
    March 1953 for a later broadcast [on the Light Programme] which apparently never
    happened – it was to be another three decades before it was broadcast for the first
    time.

(a) also arranged for symphonic wind band by Martin Ellerby, under the close guidance of
the composer (1995)
Commissioned by the USAF and "Dedicated to my dear friends, Herb and Jo Ann Stier of
San Antonio, Texas"
First performance United States Airforce Band – Chicago, USA, 20 December 1995
First UK performance European Wind Band/Rodney Parker – The Anvil, Basingstoke, 10
    February 1996
Publisher Studio Music, 1996

Concerto for oboe and string orchestra Op.39 (1952)
Commissioned by and dedicated to Léon Goossens
Duration 15'
First performance Léon Goossens/Boyd Neel Orchestra/Boyd Neel – Royal Festival Hall,
    London, 26 June 1953
First broadcast performance (regional) Léon Goossens/BBC Midland Light Orchestra/Gilbert
    Vinter – Light Programme, 7 December 1953 (from the Vestry Hall, Birmingham)
First broadcast performance (national) Léon Goossens/Boyd Neel Orchestra/Anthony Collins
    – Third Programme, 10 January 1954 (repeated on the Home Service, 21 December 1955)
Publisher Paterson, 1952, 1957 (arranged for oboe and piano)
Articles (i) Alan Poulton, 'Arnold's Whistlers' (with music example) – *Beckus* 110, Autumn
    2018
(ii) Daniel Adni, 'Malcolm Arnold's Concertos: masterpieces of melange' – *Maestro* 5,
    October 2018

Catalogue of works

Symphony No.2 Op.40 (1953)
Commissioned by the Winter Gardens Society, Bournemouth, and dedicated to Charles Groves and the Bournemouth Municipal Orchestra in celebration of their Diamond Jubilee
Duration 30'
Instrumentation 2+picc./2/2/2 + cbsn. – 4/3/3/1 – timp. perc. hp. str.
First performance Bournemouth Municipal Orchestra/Charles Groves – Winter Gardens, Bournemouth, 25 May 1953
First broadcast performance (regional) BBC Scottish Orchestra/Alexander Gibson – Scottish Home Service (from Glasgow), 28 August 1953 (repeated on the Light Programme, 7 October 1953)
First broadcast performance (national) BBC Scottish Orchestra/Alexander Gibson – BBC Third Programme, 9 February 1954
First Europe performance L'Orchestre Symphonique du Conservatoire de Grenoble/Eric-Paul Stekel – Grenoble, France, 4 March 1954
First Canada performance CBC Symphony Orchestra/John Avison – Vancouver, 26 April 1954
First London performance London Philharmonic Orchestra/Malcolm Arnold – Royal Festival Hall, London, 3 June 1954
First US performance Chicago Symphony Orchestra/Fritz Reiner – Civic Opera House, Chicago, 13 December 1956
First South Africa performance Cape Town Orchestra/Anthony Collins – Cape Town City Hall, 25 April 1957
First Australia performance Sydney Symphony Orchestra/Sir Bernard Heinze – Sydney Town Hall, 10 February 1963
First televised performance Bournemouth Symphony Orchestra/Richard Hickox – Royal Albert Hall, London, 4 September 1994 (Promenade Concert)
Publisher Paterson, 1953
Articles (i) Piers Burton-Page, 'Symphony No.2' – *Beckus* 12, March 1994; *Maestro* 1, October 2014 (Programme notes from the LSO concert conducted by Richard Hickox – Barbican, London, 8 March 1994)
(ii) Alan Poulton, 'Lamond Clelland: piccolo player' (with music examples) – *Maestro* 5, October 2018

(a) Allegro and Vivace for wind band Op.40a (2001)* arranged by Peter Parkes
Duration 11'
Publisher Novello/Studio Music
Notes *Movements 1 and 2 of Symphony No.2 Op.40

Purple Dust (1953)
[Sean O'Casey]
Instrumentation Fl. Hp. Perc. Vn. Vn. Va. Vc.
First performance Theatre Royal, Glasgow, April 1953
First London performance Lyceum Theatre, London, May 1953
    Producer: Sam Wanamaker
    Principals: Siobhan McKenna, Miles Malleson, Walter Hudd
First broadcast performance – Studio Orchestra/Michael Henry – Radio 3, 16 September 1986
    (a BBC Northern Ireland production)
    Director: Susan Hogg

First concert performance (selection of songs) Jessica Gillingwater (Sop.)/Shuang Wang
     (Pno.) – Royal & Derngate, Northampton, 21 October 2006 (First Malcolm Arnold
     Festival)
Publisher QTP
Article Anthony Meredith, 'The Purple Dust Saga' – *Beckus* 81, Summer 2011

'Katherine, Walking and Running' for two violins (1952)
Written for Katherine (Arnold), aged four, to play with a school friend
Duration 40"
First public performance Jonathan Whiting (Vn.)/Paul Harris (Vn.) – Malcolm Arnold
     Academy, Northampton, 12 October 2019 (Fourteenth Malcolm Arnold Festival)
Publisher QTP

Sonatina for recorder and piano Op.41 (1953)
Written for and dedicated to Philip Rodgers, the blind recorder player
Duration 7'45"
First performance Philip Rodgers (Rec.)/Albert Hardie (Pno.) – BBC Home Service, 14 July
     1953 (repeated on 8 June 1954)
Publisher Paterson, 1953 (also suitable for flute or oboe)

(a) arranged for recorder and string orchestra by Philip Lane (1999)
First performance John Turner (Rec.)/Royal Ballet Sinfonia/Gavin Sutherland [CD recording]
First concert performance Alison Baldwin (Rec.)/Ealing Symphony Orchestra/John Gibbons –
     St Matthew's Church, Northampton, 19 October 2013 (Eighth Malcolm Arnold Festival)
Publisher Novello, 2000 (as 'Concertino for recorder and strings Op.41a')

Homage to the Queen: Ballet Op.42 (1952)
[I. Prelude and Opening Scene
     II. 'Earth': Girl's Variation – Man's Variation – Finale
     III. 'Water': Moderato – Man's Variation – Girl's Variation – Pas de Deux
     IV. 'Fire': Pas de Deux – Girl's Variation – Man's Variation – Finale
     V. 'Air': Man's Variation – Pas de Deux
     VI. Finale 'Apotheosis']
Commissioned by the Sadler's Wells Ballet Company in honour of the Coronation of Her
Majesty Queen Elizabeth II
Duration 40'
Instrumentation 2+picc./2/2/2 – 4/3/3/1 – timp. perc.(2) cel. hp. str.
First performance Orchestra of the Royal Opera House, Covent Garden/Robert Irving – Roya
     Opera House, Covent Garden, London, 2 June 1953 (Coronation Night)
     Choreography: Frederick Ashton
     Scenery and costumes: Oliver Messel
     Lighting designer: John Sullivan
     Performers: Nadia Nerina (Queen of the Earth) and Alexis Rassine (her Consort);
     Violetta Elvin (Queen of the Water) and John Hart (her Consort); Beryl Grey (Queen
     of Fire), John Field (her Consort) and Alexander Grant (Spirit of Fire); Margot Fonteyn
     (Queen of the Air) and Michael Somes (her Consort).
Publisher Paterson, 1953

Catalogue of works

Notes (i) Humphrey Searle was initially approached but declined as he felt he could not complete the project on schedule. Despite a number of film commitments, Arnold was still able to deliver the finished score in a matter of weeks.

(ii) 'Homage to the Queen', is, in a sense, four ballets in one. Each of the four sections is a vehicle for a choreographic display by one of the Four Elements, each represented by a Queen, her Consort and an attendant Court. The ballet concludes with an apotheosis of 'homage' to Elizabeth I and the newly crowned Elizabeth II.

(iii) The first American performance was given in the Metropolitan Opera House, New York, on 18 September 1953

(iv) 'Homage to the Queen' was featured in the series 'Stories from the Ballet' adapted for broadcasting by Ursula Roseveare and narrated by Philip Cunningham – the BBC Midland Light Orchestra was conducted by Gerald Gentry and broadcast on the Home Service, 26 September 1957

(v) The ballet, with new choreography, was performed at the Royal Opera House, Covent Garden from 5-9 June 2006 (five performances)

Article Paul Jackson: 'An Original Voice Uncompromised' – *Beckus* 22, Autumn 1996; *Maestro* 1, October 2014

(a) Homage to the Queen: Ballet Suite Op.42a (1953) arranged by the composer
Duration 17'
Instrumentation 2+picc./2/2/2 – 4/3/3/1 – timp. perc.(2) cel. hp. str.
First performance London Philharmonic Orchestra/Malcolm Arnold – New Theatre, Northampton, 19 July 1953*
First broadcast performance BBC Symphony Orchestra/John Hollingsworth – Light Programme, 11 August 1956 (Promenade Concert direct from the Royal Albert Hall, London)
First Europe performance Aarhus Conservatoire Orchestra/Douglas Bostock – Aarhus, Denmark, 14 September 2001
Publisher Paterson, 1954; Novello, 2010 (study score)
Notes *There was an earlier performance of music from the ballet given at the Granada Theatre, Harrow, Middlesex by the London Symphony Orchestra conducted by Muir Mathieson on 17 June 1953 (Coronation Celebration Concert)

(b) Ballet Suite (Finale) arranged for military band by Lt Col Sir Vivian Dunn (no date)

(c) arranged for wind band by Hisaatsu Kondo (1993)
Duration 17'
First performance Japan Band Festival, 1993
First UK performance Birmingham Symphonic Winds/Keith Allen – CBSO Centre, Birmingham, 23 June 2001
Publisher Studio Music, 1993

(d) Homage to the Queen: Ballet Suite for piano solo Op.42b (1953) arranged by the composer
[I. 'Earth' II. 'Water' III. 'The Spirit of Fire' IV. 'The Queen of the Air' V. Pas de deux VI. Homage March]
Duration 9'
Publisher Paterson, 1954

Sonata No.2 for violin and piano Op.43 (1953)
Commissioned by Suzanne Rozsa and Paul Hamburger
Duration 9'
First performance Suzanne Rozsa (Vn.)/Paul Hamburger (Pno.) – Recital Room, Royal
 Festival Hall, London, 21 October 1953
First broadcast performance Marjorie Lavers (Vn.)/Ivey Dickson (Pno.) – Home Service, 18
 November 1954
First Canada performance Ruggiero Ricci (Vn.)/Rebecca Pennies (Pno.) – Victoria, British
 Columbia, July/August 1970 (In the presence of the composer)
Publisher Paterson, 1953

Flourish for a 21st birthday Op.44 (1953)
Dedicated to "Sir Adrian Boult and the London Philharmonic Orchestra in celebration of the
21st anniversary of the founding of the orchestra"
Duration 3'
Instrumentation 0/0/0/0 – 4/3 + 2 cnt./3/1 – timp. perc.(3)
First performance members of the London Philharmonic Orchestra/Sir Adrian Boult – Royal
 Albert Hall, London, 7 October 1953
Publisher Studio Music, 1986

(a) arranged for brass band by Philip Sparke (1987)
Publisher Studio Music, 1987
Notes There is another (unpublished) brass band arrangement by John Wallace (2000)

(b) arranged for six trumpets (1997)
First performance students of the Royal Northern College of Music, Manchester – Media
 Centre, University of Salford, 12 November 1997 (Arnold Awards Presentation
 Ceremony)

(c) arranged for wind band by Michael McDermott (2000)
Duration 2'
Publisher Studio Music, 2000 (as 'Flourish for a Birthday')

Concerto No.1 for flute and string orchestra Op.45 (1954)
Written for and dedicated to Richard Adeney
Duration 12'30"
First performance Richard Adeney/Boyd Neel Orchestra/John Hollingsworth – Victoria &
 Albert Museum, London, 11 April 1954
First broadcast performance Richard Adeney/London Chamber Orchestra/Anthony Bernard
 – BBC Third Programme, 3 September 1954 (repeated on the Light Programme, 30
 November 1954)
Publisher Paterson, 1954 (also arranged for flute and piano)
Article Daniel Adni, 'Malcolm Arnold's Concertos: masterpieces of mélange' (with music
 examples) – *Maestro* 5, October 2018

The Tempest (1954)
[William Shakespeare]
Instrumentation Ob. Cl. Tpt. Tbn. Perc. Hp. Timp. Glock. Cel.(Vib)

First performance Old Vic Theatre, London, 13 April 1954
Music played by: Old Vic Theatre Orchestra/Christopher Whelan
Producer: Robert Helpmann
Costumes and decor: Leslie Hurry
Principals: Michael Hordern (Prospero), Claire Bloom (Miranda), Richard Burton
(Caliban) and Robert Hardy (Ariel)
First concert performance Kathryn Knight (Sop.) and members of the Northamptonshire
County Youth Orchestra, with Robert Hardy as the Narrator – Royal & Derngate,
Northampton, 6 October 2007 (Second Malcolm Arnold Festival)
Article Michael Meredith, 'The Tempest at Eton' – Beckus 106, Autumn 2017

(a) Seven Songs from 'The Tempest' arranged for voice and piano by the composer (1954)
[Ariel's Songs: 1. Come Unto These Yellow Sands 2. Awake! 3. Where the Bee Sucks 4. Full
Fathom Five thy Father Lies; Caliban's Song: 5. Hey-Day Freedom; Stephano's Songs: 6. I
shall no more to sea 7. The Master, the swabs, the Boatswain and I (both of these songs
are unaccompanied)]

(b) Three [Ariel] Songs for unison voices and piano (no date)
[1. Come unto these yellow sands 2. Full Fathom Five thy Father lies 3. Where the bee sucks]
Duration 3'
First concert performance Choir of Old Buckenham Hall/Gordon Pullin – Old Buckenham Hall,
Suffolk, 25 May 1996
Publisher Novello/Paterson, 1959

(c) Three [Ariel] Songs arranged for unison voices and orchestra by Tobias van der Locht
(2016)
Duration 11'
Instrumentation 2+ picc./2/2/2 – 4/3/3/1 – timp.perc.(2) hp.str.
First performance Cologne University Symphony Orchestra & Chorus/Tobias van der Locht –
University Concert Hall, Cologne, Germany, 18 July 2016

(d) Suite from 'The Tempest' arranged by Thomas Nettle (2019)
First performance Tilly Goodwin and Cordelia Wood (voices)/St Andrew's Orchestra/Thomas
Nettle – Wells Cathedral School, Somerset, 9 February 2020
Articles (i) Thomas Nettle, 'Malcolm Arnold's 1954 Incidental music to The Tempest: a
proposition for a concert suite' (with music examples) – Maestro 6, October 2019
(ii) David Dunstan and Adrian Harris, 'Three Fifths in February' – Beckus 117, Summer 2020

Paddy's Nightmare: revue number (1954)
Written for the Laurier Lister entertainment 'Joyce Grenfell Requests the Pleasure'
Instrumentation Cl./Sax. Tpt. Drums Pno. Vn. Va. Vc. Db.
First London performance* Paddy Stone with the Fortune Theatre Orchestra/William Blezard
– Fortune Theatre, London, 2 June 1954
Choreography: Paddy Stone
Decor: Joan and David de Bethel, and Peter Rice
First US performance above artists – Bijou Theatre, New York, October-December 1955
Notes (i) *There had been a pre-London provincial tour taking in Cambridge, Folkestone,
Dublin and Bath
(ii) Despite extensive searches both in the UK and Canada the manuscript is still untraced.

Concerto for harmonica and orchestra Op.46 (1954)

Commissioned by the BBC for their Diamond Jubilee season of Promenade Concerts, the Concerto was written for and dedicated to Larry Adler

Duration 9'

Instrumentation 0/0/0/0 – 4/3/3/1 – timp. perc.(2) str.

First performance Larry Adler/BBC Symphony Orchestra/Malcolm Arnold* – Royal Albert Hall, London, 14 August 1954 (Promenade Concert)

First broadcast performance above performance – Light Programme, 14 August 1954 (broadcast 'live' from the Royal Albert Hall, London)

Publisher Paterson, 1954

Notes *Allegedly, Sir Malcolm Sargent had refused to conduct the concerto and Arnold took his place at the last minute.

Articles (i) Malcolm Arnold, 'Harmonica Concerto' – *Beckus* 18, Autumn 1995, *Maestro* 1, October 2014 (from 'Radio Times', March 1963)

(ii) Alan Poulton, 'Through the soloist's eyes: Harmonica Concerto', with essays on the concerto from Tommy Reilly, James Hughes, Antonio Serrano, Robert Bonfiglio and Jia-Yi He – *Maestro* 3, October 2016

(iii) Daniel Adni, 'Malcolm Arnold's Concertos: masterpieces of mélange' (with music examples) – *Maestro* 5, October 2018

Concerto for organ and orchestra Op.47 (1954)

Written for Denis Vaughan and specially composed for the organ of the Royal Festival Hall

Duration 12'30"

Instrumentation 0/0/0/0 – 0/3/0/0 – timp. str.

First performance Denis Vaughan/London Symphony Orchestra/Leslie Woodgate – Royal Festival Hall, London, 11 December 1954 (Robert Mayer Concert)

First broadcast performance Hugh McLean/London Philharmonic Orchestra/Sir Adrian Boult – Third Programme, 17 February 1957 (recorded 21 November 1955)

First Canada performance Hugh McLean/CBC Vancouver Orchestra/John Avison – Vancouver, 1970/71

First Europe performance Ulrik Spang-Hassen/Aarhus Conservatoire Orchestra/Douglas Bostock – Aarhus, Denmark 14 September 2001

Publisher Paterson, 1954

Article Alan Poulton, 'The Organ Concerto in America' – *Beckus* 106, Autumn 2017

[as a ballet] Journey: Ballet (1979)

Choreographer: Salvatore Aiello

First performance Royal Winnipeg Ballet (with Earl Stafford as the organ soloist) – Centennial Hall, Winnipeg, Canada, 2 May 1979

Articles (i) Alan Poulton, 'Arnold's other ballets' – *Maestro* 4, October 2017

(ii) 'The Richmond Ballet perform 'Journey'' – *Beckus* 108, Spring 2018

Sinfonietta No.1 for chamber orchestra Op.48 (1954)

Dedicated to the Boyd Neel Orchestra

Duration 12'

Instrumentation 0/2/0/0 – 2/0/0/0 – str.

First performance Boyd Neel Orchestra/Anthony Collins – Albert Hall, Nottingham, 3 December 1954

Catalogue of works

First London performance Boyd Neel Orchestra/Anthony Collins – Royal Festival Hall, London, 7 March 1955
First UK broadcast performance Francis Chagrin Ensemble/Francis Chagrin – BBC Home Service, 11 April 1957 (there had been an earlier [first] broadcast on French Radio)
Publisher Paterson, 1955
Article Piers Burton-Page, 'Three's company: the Sinfoniettas' – *Beckus* 98, Autumn 2015

Rinaldo and Armida: Ballet Op.49 (1954)

Written for the Sadler's Wells Ballet Company
Duration 23'
Instrumentation 2+picc./2/2/2 – 4/3/3/1 – timp. perc.(2) cel. hp. str.
First performance Orchestra of the Royal Opera House, Covent Garden/Malcolm Arnold – Royal Opera House, Covent Garden, London, 6 January 1955
    Choreography: Frederick Ashton
    Scenery and costumes: Peter Rue
    Principals: Michael Somes, Svetlana Beriosova, Julia Farron
First US performance Sadler's Wells Ballet – New York, 20 September 1955
First broadcast performance BBC Northern Symphony Orchestra/Malcolm Arnold – Radio3, 6 November 1971
First Europe performance Aarhus Conservatoire Orchestra/Douglas Bostock – Aarhus, Denmark, 14 September 2001
First London concert performance Kensington Symphony Orchestra/Russell Keable – St John's Smith Square, London, 3 July 2017
First New Zealand performance Southern Ballet Theatre – Isaac Theatre Royal, Christchurch, 14 December 2018
Publisher Faber, 1984
Article Paul Jackson 'A Serious Error' – *Beckus* 23, Winter 1996, *Maestro* 1, October 2014

(a) Excerpt 'Introduction and Pas-de-deux' arranged by Christopher Palmer (1991)
Duration 9'
First concert performance BBC Concert Orchestra/Barry Wordsworth – Queen Elizabeth Hall, London, 26 October 1991 (70th Birthday Concert)
Publisher Faber

(b) Excerpt 'Introduction and Pas-de-deux' arranged for piano sextet by Mark Underwood (2001)
Instrumentation Fl. Ob. Cl. Bsn. Hn. Pno.
First performance Harlequin – Purcell Room, London, 8 July 2001
Unpublished

(c) Excerpts arranged by the composer for solo piano
First concert performance Moritz Ernst – Royal & Derngate, Northampton – 16 October 2010 (Fifth Malcolm Arnold Festival)

War in the Air: BBC Television Service with the Air Ministry (1954-55)

Titles and transmission dates of the 15 films in the series which were scored by Malcolm Arnold were as follows:
    No.1 'The Fated Sky' (8 November 1954)
    No.4 'Maximum Effort' (29 November 1954)

No.10 'Operation Overlord' (10 January 1955)
Instrumentation (No.1) 2/1/2/1 – 4/3/3/1 – timp.perc.str
Director and commentary writer: John Elliott
Editor: Jim Pople
Music played by: London Symphony Orchestra/Muir Mathieson
Article Alan Poulton, 'Arnold on the Small Screen' – *Maestro* 6, October 2019

Serenade for guitar and string orchestra Op.50 (1955)
Written for and dedicated to Julian Bream
Duration 5'30"
First performance Julian Bream/Richmond Community Centre String Orchestra*/Malcolm
   Arnold – Richmond Community Centre Hall, Richmond, Surrey, Summer 1955
First London performance Julian Bream/Kalmar Chamber Orchestra/Leonard Friedman –
   Wigmore Hall, London, 11 June 1956
First broadcast performance Julian Bream/BBC Concert Orchestra/Vilem Tausky – Home
   Service, 25 August 1957 (repeated on 5 December 1958)
Publisher Paterson, 1955 (also arranged for guitar and piano, 1977)
Notes *Arnold's first wife, Sheila, was leader of the orchestra
Articles (i) David Dunstan, 'The elusive Serenade for Guitar and Strings' – *Beckus* 95, Winter
   2014
(ii) Piers Burton-Page, 'Malcolm Arnold and Julian Bream' – *Maestro* 7, October 2020

Tam O'Shanter: Overture for orchestra Op.51 (1955)
Dedicated to Michael Diack (Arnold's publisher and amateur horn player)
Duration 7'30"
Instrumentation 2+picc./2/2/2 – 4/3/3/1 – timp. perc.(2) str.
First performance Royal Philharmonic Orchestra/Malcolm Arnold – Royal Albert Hall,
   London, 16 August 1955 (Promenade Concert)
First broadcast performance above performance – Light Programme, 16 August 1955
   (broadcast 'live' from the Royal Albert Hall, London – repeated on 15 September 1955)
First Scotland performance Scottish National Orchestra/Alexander Gibson – Usher Hall,
   Edinburgh, 23 March 1956 (the performance was encored)
First US performance Hallé Orchestra/Sir John Barbirolli – January 1959 (during a tour of
   many of the major American cities)
First televised performance Philharmonia Orchestra/Sir Adrian Boult – BBC Television, 14
   January 1964 (direct from the Fairfield Halls, Croydon)
First Russia performance BBC Symphony Orchestra/Sir John Barbirolli – Grand Hall,
   Leningrad, 15 January 1967 (a Soviet Radio broadcast on behalf of the State Leningrad
   Academic Philharmonic Society and broadcast 'live' on Network 3 in the UK)
First South Africa performance Natal Philharmonic Orchestra – Natal, October 1987
Publisher Paterson, 1955
Notes (i) The Overture takes its name from the work that inspired it, the narrative poem by
   Robert Burns, the introduction to which is printed on the cover of the score.
(ii) In the early nineties the famous Scottish actor John Cairney, developed a stage musical
   play using the music of the Overture (with Sir Malcolm's permission). In 1994 the
   musical play was performed by Radio New Zealand (Producer: John O'Leary) and for

which it received the Mobil Oil Award. The play was later taken to New York in 1996 where it received the New York Critics Award.

Article Frank Brand, 'Tam O'Shanter – the play' – *Beckus* 96, Spring 2015

(a) arranged for wind band by John Paynter (1991)
Publisher Carl Fischer (New York)

(b) arranged for brass band by Howard Snell (2001)
Publisher Studio Music
Notes There is another (unpublished) brass band arrangement by Alan Catherall

Electra: incidental music (1955)

[Sophocles trans. Edward Fairchild Watling: 1. Prelude 2. Electra's Entrance 3. Lamentation 4. Aegisthus and Clytemnestra 5. Postlude]
Instrumentation Fl. Perc.
Music played by: Christopher Hyde-Smith (Fl.) and James Wolfenden (Perc.)
First performance Borough Polytechnic Players – Edric Hall, Borough Polytechnic, London, 7 December 1955
　　Producers: Thomas Vaughan and Donald Bisset
　　Principals: Thomas Vaughan, Monica Evans*, Margaret Davies
First modern performance Pam Carter (Fl.)/Tim Green (Perc.) – Malcolm Arnold Academy, Northampton, 12 October 2019 (Fourteenth Malcolm Arnold Festival)
Notes *Over six decades later, the 80-year-old Monica Evans was in attendance at the first modern performance of Arnold's incidental music.
Article David Dunstan, '14th Arnold Festival' – *Beckus* 115, Winter 2019

Fanfare for a Festival, for brass and percussion (1955)

Originally written for the 1955 Hastings Festival
Duration 2'
Instrumentation 4 Hn. 3 Tpt. Cnt. 3 Tbn. Tba. Timp. Perc.(3)
First performance members of the London Philharmonic Orchestra/Sir Adrian Boult – White Rock Pavilion, Hastings, 4 May 1956
First modern performance members of the Brighton Philharmonic Orchestra/Barry Wordsworth – Brighton Dome, 25 March 2018
Publisher Studio Music, 1986
Notes The Fanfare includes a quotation from the song 'Sussex by the Sea' written in 1907 by William Ward-Higgs, a resident of Bexhill. It has now become the unofficial march of the Royal Sussex Regiment. Arnold had originally suggested an orchestration of the song for the 1955 Festival of Music but this never materialised.
Article Alan Poulton, 'Brighton Philharmonic Orchestra' – *Beckus* 108, Spring 2018

(a) arranged for brass band by Philip Sparke (1986)
First performance Band of the Royal Military School of Music, Kneller Hall/Lt Col Duncan Beat – Royal Albert Hall, London, 4 October 1986 (National Brass Band Championships Festival Concert)
Publisher Studio Music, 1986

(b) arranged for military/wind band by Michael McDermott (2000)
First broadcast performance Central Band of the Royal Air Force/Wing Commander Eric
  Banks – Radio 3, 9 April 1987
Publisher Studio Music, 2000

John Clare Cantata for SATB chorus and piano duet Op.52 (1955)
[1. Winter Snow Storm 2. March 3. Spring 4. Summer 5. Autumn 6. Epilogue]
Duration 11'
Commissioned by William Glock for the 1955 Dartington Summer School of Music
First performance Dartington Summer School Choir/Viola Tunnard and Martin Penny (piano
  duet)/John Clements – Dartington Hall, Totnes, South Devon, 5 August 1955 (Dartington
  Summer School Concert)
First broadcast performance BBC Chorus/Viola Tunnard and Martin Penny (piano duet)/
  Alexander Gibson – BBC Third Programme, 16 April 1956
First modern Europe performance Via-Nova-Chor Munchen/Duo d'Accord/Florian Helgarth –
  Musikhochschule München, Germany, 1 November 2014
Publisher Paterson, 1956

**(a) John Clare Cantata for chorus and string orchestra Op.52a (2015) arranged by John
  Gibbons**
First performance The Goodwine Choir/strings of the Birmingham Conservatoire Orchestra/
  Alex Davan Wetton – St Matthew's Church, Northampton, 17 October 2015 (Tenth
  Malcolm Arnold Festival)

Little Suite No.1 for orchestra Op.53 (1955)
[1. Prelude 2. Dance 3. March]
Originally written for the National Youth Orchestra of Great Britain and entitled 'To Youth'
Suite (q.v.), it was revised with a change of central movement title from 'Pastoral' to
'Dance'
Duration 9'30"
Instrumentation 2/2/2/2 – 4/3/3/1 – timp. perc.(2) str.
First performance (rev. version) Schools' Music Association Orchestra/Malcolm Arnold –
  Royal Albert Hall, London, April 1955 (Schools' Music Association Concert)
First broadcast performance BBC Midland Orchestra/Gerald Gentry – Home Service, 20
  February 1958
Publisher Paterson, 1956

(a) arranged for wind band by Denis Bloodworth (1988)
Publisher Molenaar, 1988

(b) arranged for brass band by Robin Norman (2007)
First concert performance Ipswich and Norwich Co-op Band/Robin Norman – Royal &
  Derngate, Northampton, 25 October 2009 (Fourth Malcolm Arnold Festival)
Publisher Feldman, as 'Prelude, Dance and March Op.53a'

(c) arranged for recorder orchestra by Denis Bloodworth (with Little Suite No.2 Op.78)
First performance London Recorder Orchestra/Denis Bloodworth – summer concert, 1996
Unpublished

(d) Excerpt No.3 – March, arranged for military band by Peter Sumner (1965)
Duration 2'30"
Publisher Novello/Paterson; Carl Fisher (New York), 1965

(e) Excerpt No.3 – March, arranged for brass band by Neil Richmond (2002)
First performance Harrogate Band – St John's College, York, 9 March 2003
Unpublished

Candlemas Night: a fantastic comedy, music for radio (1955)
[Ernest Reynolds]
Duration 15'
Instrumentation Picc. 2 Fl. Tpt. Timp. Perc. Hp. Cel.
Music played by: Chamber Ensemble/Lionel Salter (recorded 18 November 1955)
First performance BBC Third Programme, 25 December 1955 (and repeated on 26 February 1956)
  Producer: Frederick Bradnum
  Principals: Vivienne Bennett, Gordon Davies, Freda Jackson, Hamilton Dyce
Article Alan Poulton, 'Music for Candlemas Night' (with music example) – *Beckus* 118, Autumn 2020

Piano Trio Op.54 (1956)
Dedicated to Pauline Howgill, the founder of the St Cecilia Trio
Duration 12'30"
Instrumentation Vn. Vc. Pno.
First performance St Cecilia Trio – Sylvia Cleaver (Vn.)/Norman Jones (Vc.)/Pauline Howgill (Pno.) – International Music Association, London, 30 April 1956
First broadcast performance above performance – BBC Home Service, 7 September 1956
Publisher Paterson, 1956

Song of Praise for unison voices and piano (or orchestra) Op.55 (1956)
[Words: John Clare]
Commissioned by Ruth Railton for the Jubilee of Wycombe Abbey School for Girls, High Wycombe
Duration 4'
Instrumentation 1/1/1/1 – 2/2/2/0 – timp. perc. org. str.
Alt instrumentation pno. str.
First performance Pupils of Wycombe Abbey School for Girls/Ruth Railton – Wycombe Abbey, 6 July 1956 (Wycombe Abbey School's Jubilee Speech Day)
First modern performance Festival Singers/Bernard West – St Matthew's Church, Northampton, 18 October 2008 (Third Malcolm Arnold Festival)
Publisher Paterson, 1956

Solitaire: Ballet (1956)
Written for the Sadler's Wells Ballet Company, the music comprises the earlier sets of English Dances (in a new order) and two newly-composed dances – Sarabande and Polka.
Duration 25'30"
Instrumentation 2+picc./2/2/2 – 4/2/2/0 – timp. perc.(2) cel. hp. str.

First performance Sadler's Wells Theatre Orchestra/John Lanchberry – Sadler's Wells
Theatre, London, 7 June 1956
Choreography: Kenneth MacMillan
Scenery: Desmond Heeley
Principals: Margaret Hill, Donald McLeary, Michael Boulton, Donald Britton
First US performance Sadler's Wells Ballet – New York, 17 September 1957 (with Anya Linden
in the leading role)
First Europe performance Stuttgart Ballet, 1960
Publisher Lengnick, 1956
Article Tony Meredith, 'Solitaire: sixty years on' – *Beckus* 102, Autumn 2016

(a) arranged for small orchestra by Philip Lane (2005)
Instrumentation 1+picc./2/1/0 – 2/2/2/0 – timp.perc.hp.cel. str.
First performance Birmingham Royal Ballet/Royal Ballet Sinfonia/Paul Murphy – Birmingham
Hippodrome, 5 October 2005
First London performance Sadler's Wells, 25 October 2005

(b) Excerpt Sarabande and Polka, for orchestra (1959)
Duration 8'30"
First concert performance BBC Concert Orchestra/Malcolm Arnold – BBC General Overseas
Service, 15 February 1960 (repeated on the Home Service, 25 March 1963)

(c) Excerpt Sarabande and Polka, arranged for piano solo by the composer (1959)
First concert performance Moritz Ernst – Royal & Derngate, Northampton, 16 October 2010
(Fifth Malcolm Arnold Festival)
Publisher Paterson, 1959; Yorktown Music Press/Music Sales Ltd, in 'The Joy of More English
Music for piano'

(d) Excerpt Sarabande and Polka, arranged for wind band by John Paynter (1983)
Publisher Novello/Paterson; Carl Fischer (New York)

(e) Excerpt Sarabande and Polka, arranged for brass band (no date)

(f) Excerpt Sarabande, arranged for flute and piano by Alan Poulton (1984)
First performance John Franklin (Fl.)/Alan Poulton (Pno.) – The Yett, Hopton Bank, Cleobury
Mortimer, Shropshire, 7 July 1984 (in the presence of the composer)
First performance (version for clarinet and piano) Linda Merrick (Cl.)/Benjamin Frith
(Pno.) – Darwin Suite, Assembly Rooms, Derby, 24 June 1994 (Jeffery Tillett Concert in
association with Derby City Council)
Publisher Novello, 2004

Fanfare for a Royal Occasion (1956)
Written for the opening of the 1956 St Cecilia's Day Concert
Duration 1'30"
Instrumentation 3 Tpt. 3 Tbn.
First performance Trumpeters of the Royal Military School of Music, Kneller Hall/Lt Col David
McBain – Royal Festival Hall, London, 19 November 1956 (St Cecilia's Day Concert on
behalf of the Musicians' Benevolent Fund)
Publisher Studio Music, 1986 (as No.4 of 'Four Fanfares')

Notes This concert was attended by Her Majesty Queen Elizabeth the Queen Mother and televised by the BBC.

The Open Window: Opera in one Act Op.56 (1956)
[Libretto: Sidney Gilliat based on a short story by H H Munro (Saki)*]
Commissioned by BBC Television
Duration 30'
Instrumentation Fl. Cl. Bsn. Hn. Hp. Perc. Vn.(2) Va. Vc. Db.
First performance BBC Television production, 14 December 1956
    Music played by: English Opera Group Orchestra/Lionel Salter
    Principals: John Carolan (Mr Nuttel), June Bronhill (Vera), Flora Nielsen (Alice
    Sappleton) and Ethel Lyon (The Maid)
    Producer: George R Fox
    Designer: Richard Wilmot
First public performance (staged with piano) Lincoln Opera Group/Lionel Barnby – Horton-
    cum-Beckering Country Theatre, Lincolnshire, April 1958
First public performance (staged with orchestra) Morley College Opera Group/Morley
    Chamber Orchestra/Harry Samuel – Morley College, London, 18 December 1961 (a
    'double bill' with *Ghost Story* by James Stevens)
First modern performance (concert version with piano) Soloists of Trinity College of Music,
    London with David Knotts (piano) – Royal & Derngate, Northampton, 18 October 2008
    (Third Malcolm Arnold Festival)
    Principals: Charmian Bedford (Vera), Belinda Williams (Alice Sappleton), Simon Iorio (Mr
    Nuttel) and Sophie Bibuyck (The Maid)
    Director: Linda Hurst
First modern performance (semi-staged version with orchestra) Soloists/Berkeley Ensemble/
    Dominic Grier – St Matthew's Church, Northampton, 18 October 2014 (Ninth Malcolm
    Arnold Festival)
    Principals: Caroline Kennedy (Vera), Anna Huntley (Alice Sappleton/The Maid), Ben
    Thapa (Mr Nuttel)
Publisher Novello (full and vocal score); Novello, (Excerpts in 'Malcolm Arnold: Songs and
    Arias' – 1. Mr Nuttel's aria 2. Vera's aria)
Notes *The story was first published in *Beasts and Super Beasts* in 1914
Articles (i) Piers Burton-Page, 'A Window Opens' – *Beckus* 71, Winter 2008; *Maestro* 6,
    October 2019
(ii) Alan Poulton, 'Up at the Villa – Appendix 1' – *Beckus* 101, Summer 2016

A Grand, Grand (Festival) Overture for orchestra Op.57 (1956)
Written for the Hoffnung Music Festival – the score bears a dedication to President Hoover
Duration 8'
Instrumentation 2+picc./2/2/2 – 4/3/3/1 – timp. perc.(2) org. str. (+ 3 vacuum cleaners, 1 floor
    polisher and 4 rifles)
First performance Morley College Symphony Orchestra/Malcolm Arnold with Dennis Brain
    (organ) – Royal Festival Hall, London, 13 November 1956 (Hoffnung Music Festival)*
First Australia performance Sydney Symphony Orchestra/John Farnsworth Hall – Sydney
    Town Hall, 12 November 1958 (and repeated on 13 and 14 November as the concluding
    concert of the 1958 series of Youth Concerts)

Publisher Paterson, 1956
Notes *Transmitted 'live' from the Royal Festival Hall on BBC Television

(a) arranged for symphonic wind band by Keith Wilson (1983)
Publisher Paterson; Carl Fischer (New York), 1983

(b) arranged for military band by Major Rodney Bashford (c.1970)
First broadcast performance Band of the Grenadier Guards/Major Rodney Bashford – Radio
 3, 26 January 1970
Notes Muted cornets substitute for the floor polisher in this arrangement!

(c) arranged for brass band by David Richards (1988)
First concert performance Ipswich and Norwich Co-op Band/Robin Norman – Royal &
 Derngate, Northampton, 25 October 2009 (Fourth Malcolm Arnold Festival)
Publisher Paterson/Novello, 1988
Notes There is also another (unpublished) arrangement for brass band by Ray Farr (1985)

The ABC March (Fanfare): ABC titles (1956)
Written for the launch of the ABC Television Network in 1956
Duration 1'30"
Music played by: Orchestra/Muir Mathieson
Article Alan Poulton, 'The ABC March (Fanfare)' – *Beckus* 96, Spring 2015

Concerto No.2 for horn and string orchestra Op.58 (1956)
Written for and dedicated to Dennis Brain
Duration 13'30"
First performance Dennis Brain/Hallé Orchestra/Malcolm Arnold – Cheltenham Town Hall, 17
 July 1957 (Cheltenham Festival)
First broadcast performance Barry Tuckwell/BBC Scottish Orchestra/Bryden Thomson –
 Network 3,17 October 1966 (repeated on the NI Home Service, 17 November 1967)
First London performance Alan Civil/English Chamber Orchestra/Malcolm Arnold –
 Bishopsgate Institute, London, 3 March 1969
First Europe broadcast performance Barry Tuckwell/Netherlands Radio Orchestra/Kenneth
 Montgomery – May 1978 (and broadcast in the UK (Radio 4), 4 August 1978)
Publisher Paterson, 1956
Articles (i) William C. Lynch, 'Brothers in Brass: the friendship of Malcolm Arnold and Dennis
 Brain' (with music examples) – *Maestro* 2, October 2015
(ii) Frank Lloyd, 'Second horn concerto' – *Maestro* 3, October 2016
(iii) Alan Poulton, 'Horn Concerto No.2: how the manuscript got to the USA' – *Beckus* 118,
 Autumn 2020

(a) arranged for horn and piano by Julian Elloway (1988)
Publisher Novello, 1988

Four Scottish Dances for orchestra Op.59 (1957)
[1. Strathspey 2. Reel* 3. Hebridean (Waltz) 4. Highland Fling]
Commissioned by the BBC for their Light Music Festival to whom the work is dedicated
Duration 8'30"
Instrumentation 1+picc./2/2/2 – 4/2/3/0 – timp. perc. hp. str.

Catalogue of works

First performance BBC Concert Orchestra/Malcolm Arnold – Royal Festival Hall, London, 8 June 1957 (BBC Light Music Festival)
First Scotland performance Scottish National Orchestra/Alexander Gibson – c.1958
First Europe performance Kraków Philharmonic Orchestra – Poland, 24 May 1998
Publisher Paterson, 1957
Notes *The reel is a tune dating from 1796 attributed to Robert Burns and entitled 'We'll Gang Nae Mair to Yon Town' which Arnold had first used in the 1949 documentary film 'The Fair County of Ayr'.
Article Alan Poulton, 'The Fair County of Ayr' (with music examples) – *Beckus* 109, Summer 2018

(a) arranged for symphonic wind band by John Paynter
First Scotland performance Massed Bands/Ben Gernon – Pickaquoy Centre, Kirkwall, 21 June 2011 (St Magnus International Festival)
Publisher Novello/Paterson; Carl Fischer (New York)
Notes John Paynter (1928-1996) was President of the National Band Association of America and for 45 years the Director of Bands at Northwestern University. The Indianapolis Wind Symphony conducted by Charles Conrad, performed Paynter's transcription in Indianapolis on 14 October 2001 in honour of the composer's 80th birthday.

(b) arranged for brass band by Ray Farr (1984)
First performance Manger Brass Band/Michael Antrobus – Usher Hall, Edinburgh, 6 May 1984
First England performance Salford College of Technology Brass Band/David King – University of Salford, 20 November 1991 (Arnold/Haydn Celebrations)
First London performance Grimethorpe Colliery Band/Elgar Howarth – Queen Elizabeth Hall, London, 27 September 2004
Publisher Novello/Paterson, 1984

(c) arranged for violin and piano by David Gedge (2004)
Publisher Novello, 2004
Notes There is another (unpublished) version of Dance No.3 for violin and piano, made by Janet Packer and performed by her in the USA in 1996

(d) arranged for piano solo by John York (2003)
First London performance Moritz Ernst – St Paul's Church, Covent Garden, 5 June 2007
Publisher Novello, 2003

(e) No.3, arranged for piano solo by Stephen Duro
Publisher Chester, 1997 (in 'Contemporary Classics' No.1)

[as a ballet] Flowers of the Forest: Ballet (1985)
First performance Birmingham Royal Ballet – Birmingham Hippodrome, 14 June 1985
First London performance above artists/Royal Ballet Sinfonia/Bramwell Tovey – Sadler's Wells Theatre, London, 24 September 1985
First US performance above artists – Brooklyn Academy of Music, 6 February 1986
Choreography: David Bintley, and dedicated to his wife Jenny and son Michael.
Notes (i) Conceived as two Scottish ballets danced to both Arnold's music and to Britten's 'Scottish Ballad', the title is taken from the famous ballad which mourns the death of Scottish youth at the Battle of Flodden Field in 1513.

(ii) Arnold's Four Scottish Dances were first used as a ballet in 1979 for a Sadler's
   Wells overseas tour of Israel – at the request of Vyvyan Lorraine and with original
   choreography by David Bintley (see also Appendix A)
Article Alan Poulton, 'Flowers of the Forest' (Birmingham Royal Ballet) – *Beckus* 95, Winter
   2014

HRH The Duke of Cambridge: march for military band Op.60 (1957)
Written to celebrate the centenary of the Royal Military School of Music, Kneller Hall and
dedicated to Lt Col David McBain
Duration 3'30"
First performance Band of the Royal Military School of Music/Lt Col David McBain – Kneller
   Hall, Twickenham, Middlesex, 26 May 1957 (an Open Air Concert televised 'live' on BBC
   Television, and introduced by Franklin Engelmann)*
First broadcast performance Band of the Grenadier Guards/Major Rodney Bashford – Radio
   3, 9 September 1968
Publisher Paterson/Carl Fischer (New York), 1957
Notes (i) HRH Duke of Cambridge was the Commander in Chief of the British Army who
   founded Kneller Hall in 1857 and who is said to have taken his title from the public house
   at the Hall's main gates.
(ii) *A month later the Band of the Royal Military School of Music, conducted by Rodney
   Bashford, gave a second performance of the March during a garden party attended by
   both Her Majesty the Queen and the composer on 28 June 1957

(a) HRH The Duke of Cambridge: march for large orchestra Op.60a (2000) arranged by
   Philip Lane
Instrumentation 1+picc./2/2/2+cbsn. – 4/3/3/1 – perc.(2) str.
First performance Bart's Festival Orchestra/John Lumley – Millennium Dome, London, 21
   October 2000 (Malcolm Arnold Birthday Concert)
Publisher Novello/Paterson

For Mr Pye, an Island (1957)
[Mervyn Peake (based on incidents from his novel 'Mr. Pye'*)]
Duration 60'
Instrumentation 2 Fl. Cl. Bcl. Tpt. Perc. Hp. Pno. Cel. Db.
Music played by: Chamber Ensemble/Malcolm Arnold
First performance BBC Home Service, 10 July 1957
   Producer: Francis Dillon
   Principals: Oliver Burt (as Mr Pye) and Betty Hardy (as Miss Dredger)
First concert performance Royal & Derngate Actors Company/Chamber Ensemble/Paul
   Truman – Royal & Derngate, Northampton, 14 October 2017 (Twelfth Malcolm Arnold
   Festival)
   Director: Trudy Bell
   Principals: Keith Maddern (Mr Pye) and Meryl Couper (Miss Dredger)
Notes *An adaptation of the book was made for Channel 4 Television by Donald Churchill in
   1986 and starred Derek Jacobi as Mr Pye.
Article Piers Burton-Page, 'An Arnold mystery island?' – *Beckus* 102, Autumn 2016

Oboe Quartet Op.61 (1957)
Written for and dedicated to Léon Goossens on the occasion of his sixtieth birthday
Duration 12'45"
Instrumentation Ob. Vn. Va. Vc.
First performance Léon Goossens/Carter String Trio – Mary Carter (Vn.), Anatole Mines (Va.), Eileen McCarthy (Vc.) – Cambridge University Music School, 2 May 1957
First broadcast performance above artists – BBC Third Programme, 18 June 1958
First London performance London Oboe Quartet: Janet Craxton (Ob.), Perry Hart (Vn.), Brian Hawkins (Va.), Charles Tunnell (Vc.) – c.July 1970
Publisher Faber, 1966
Notes Originally entitled 'Serenade for Oboe Quartet' and with 14 bars of a totally different opening crossed out.
Article Michael Jameson: 'New recording of the Oboe Quartet' – *Beckus* 99, Winter 2015

Toy Symphony Op.62 (1957)
Dedicated to the Musicians' Benevolent Fund
Duration 9'30"
Instrumentation Pno. Vn. Vn. Va. Vc. (+ 12 toy wind and percussion instruments)
First performance Soloists/Amici String Quartet/Joseph Cooper (Pno.)/Malcolm Arnold – Savoy Hotel, London, 28 November 1957 (St Cecilia Festival Dinner)
First public performance Liverpool Music Group/Fritz Speigl – New Shakespeare Theatre, Liverpool, 15 December 1957
First broadcast performance members of the BBC Scottish Orchestra/Colin Davis – Scottish Home Service, 12 May 1958 (from Glasgow) and repeated on the Light Programme, 17 December 1960
Publisher Paterson, 1958
Articles (i) Alan Poulton, 'Arnold's Shortest Symphony: The Toy Symphony' (with music examples) – *Maestro* 5, October 2018
(ii) Bernard Hughes, 'First recording of the Toy Symphony' – *Beckus* 115, Winter 2019
(iii) David Dunstan, 'At last, the Toy Symphony!' – *Beckus* 116, Spring 2020

[as a children's ballet] Bertram Batell's Sideshow: Ballet (1970) [third movement used as the Finale]
Choreography: Jonathan Taylor
First performance Ballet Rambert – Jeannetta Cochrane Theatre, London, 12 April 1971
First televised performance above – BBC 2, 27 December 1977
Notes 'Bertram Batell' is an anagram of 'Ballet Rambert'

Symphony No.3 Op.63 (1957)
Commissioned by and dedicated to the Royal Liverpool Philharmonic Society
Duration 32'30"
Instrumentation 2+picc./2/2/2 – 4/3/3/1 – timp. str.
First performance Royal Liverpool Philharmonic Orchestra/John Pritchard – Royal Festival Hall, London, 2 December 1957
First Liverpool performance above artists – Liverpool Philharmonic Hall, 10 December 1957
First broadcast performance above artists – Home Service, 25 April 1958
Publisher Paterson, 1958

Article Terry Cushion, 'Essex Symphony Orchestra', review of the Third Symphony (and Flourish for orchestra), Chelmsford, 26 November 2016 – *Beckus* 104, Spring 2017

Commonwealth Christmas Overture for orchestra Op.64 (1957)

Commissioned by the BBC for the 1959 'Christmas Round the World' programme celebrating the 25th anniversary of the first Christmas broadcast by a British monarch (King George V in 1932)
Duration 14'30"
Instrumentation 2+picc./2/2/2 – 4/3/3/1 – timp. perc.(4) cel. hp. str. (+ 3 guitars, and an Afro-Cuban percussion group (4) – marimba, maracas, bongos and conga))
First performance BBC Symphony Orchestra/Rudolf Schwarz – BBC, 25 December 1957
First concert performance London Symphony Orchestra/Alexander Gibson – date unknown
First US performance Carmel Symphony Orchestra – Carmel, Indiana, 12 December 2009
Publisher Lengnick, 1991

Royal Prologue: Crown and Commonwealth: BBC radio (1957)

[Christopher Hassall]
Commissioned by the BBC
Duration 31'
Instrumentation 1/1/2/0 – 1/2/1/0 – timp. perc. hp. pno. str.
Music played by: Trumpeters of the Royal Military School of Music, Kneller Hall/Royal Philharmonic Orchestra/Malcolm Arnold, with Sir William McKie (organ) – BBC, 25 December 1957
Narrator: Sir Laurence Olivier
Producer: Rex Moorfoot

Richmond Fanfare for brass (1957)

Originally commissioned by the BBC as part of the Royal Prologue music where the Fanfare trumpeters were conducted by Lt Col David McBain
Duration 36"
Instrumentation 3 Tpt. 3 Tbn.
First concert performance Fanfare trumpeters of the Royal Military School of Music, Kneller Hall/Major Rodney Bashford – Richmond, Surrey, Christmas 1957
First broadcast performance above performance – 2 April 1962
Publisher Studio Music, 1986 (as No.2 of 'Four Fanfares')
Notes This Fanfare was played during the Olympic Parade in London on 10 September 2012

Concert Piece for percussion (1958)

Originally written for BBC Television and dedicated to James Blades – the score is dated 1 June 1958
Duration 4'30"
Instrumentation Pno. Timp.(3) Perc.(3)
First performance 'Music Makers – No.6 Percussion'* – BBC Television, 28 October 1960
Producer: John Hosier
Publisher Faber, 1984
Notes *James Blades did not take part in the TV premiere which was performed by three percussionists and piano – the date has not been verified.

Catalogue of works

Articles (i) Alan Poulton, 'Concert Piece for Percussion' (this includes an essay by Evelyn
Glennie entitled 'The Concert Piece – a little gem') – *Beckus* 110, Autumn 2018
(ii) Alan Poulton, 'Arnold on the Small Screen' – *Maestro* 6, October 2019

arranged by James Blades as: Concert Piece for percussion and piano (1961)
First performance James Blades (Perc.)/Joan Goossens (Pno.) – Grendon Hall, Northants, 6
December 1961 (though another source cites an earlier date of 17 December 1959)
First broadcast performance above artists – BBC Music Programme, 30 December 1966
Publisher Faber, 1984 (for one or two percussion players)

Music for You: signature tune for BBC Television series (1958)
Duration 2'30"
Instrumentation 2 + picc./2/2/2 + cbsn. – 4/3/3/1 – timp. perc. hp. str.
First performance Eric Robinson Orchestra – BBC Television, 22 March 1959 (first
transmission date using Arnold's tune)

Sinfonietta No.2 for chamber orchestra Op.65 (1958)
Written for the 21st anniversary of the Jacques Orchestra and dedicated to Reginald
Jacques
Duration 12'30"
Instrumentation 2/0/0/0 – 2/0/0/0 – str.
First performance Jacques Orchestra/Reginald Jacques – Victoria & Albert Museum, London,
15 June 1958
First broadcast performance above performance – Home Service, 15 July 1959 (repeated on
the Scottish Home Service, 14 November 1960)
Publisher Paterson, 1958
Article Piers Burton-Page, 'Three's company: the Sinfoniettas' – *Beckus* 98, Autumn 2015

United Nations for 4 military bands, organ and orchestra (1958)
Commissioned for the 1958 Hoffnung Interplanetary Music Festival
Duration 13'
Instrumentation picc.+2/2/2/2 – 4/3/3/1 – timp. perc.(3) str.
First performance Band of the Royal Military School of Music, Kneller Hall/Morley College
Symphony Orchestra/Malcolm Arnold – Royal Festival Hall, London, 21 November 1958
(Hoffnung Interplanetary Music Festival)

Five William Blake Songs for contralto and string orchestra Op.66 (1959)
[1. O Holy Virgin! Clad in purest white
2. Memory hither come and tune your merry notes
3. How sweet I roam'd from field to field
4. My silks and fine array
5. Thou Fair-hair'd angel of the evening]
Written for Pamela Bowden
Duration 13'30"
First performance Pamela Bowden/Richmond Community Centre String Orchestra/Malcolm
Arnold – Richmond Community Centre Hall, Richmond, Surrey, 26 March 1959
First London performance Pamela Bowden/Jacques Orchestra/Reginald Jacques – Victoria &
Albert Museum, London, 12 July 1959

First broadcast performance Pamela Bowden/BBC Northern Orchestra/Malcolm Arnold –
  Third Programme, 28 January 1966 (Manchester Midday Prom Concert)
First performance (version for high voice and piano) Jessica Gillingwater (Sop.)/Shuang
  Wang (Pno.) – Royal & Derngate, Northampton, 21 October 2006 (First Malcolm Arnold
  Festival)
Publisher British & Continental Music Agency, 1966; Novello, in 'Malcolm Arnold: Songs and
  Arias' (arranged for voice and piano)

Four Pieces for chamber ensemble (1959)
[1. Prelude 2. Waltz 3. Chorale 4. Carillon]
Written for the Arnold family* to play as practice pieces
Instrumentation Vn.(2) Fl. Rec.
Notes *Malcolm and Sheila (Vns.); Katherine (Fl.) and Robert (Rec.)

Concerto for guitar and chamber ensemble (or orchestra) Op.67 (1959)
Commissioned by and dedicated to Julian Bream (the second movement is dedicated to the
memory of Django Reinhardt)
Duration 21'30"
Instrumentation Fl. Cl. Hn. Vn.(2) Va. Vc. Db.
Alt instrumentation 1/0/1/0 – 1/0/0/0 – str.
First performance Julian Bream/Melos Ensemble/Malcolm Arnold – BBC Third Programme,
  18 June 1959 (repeated on the Home Service, 12 August 1961)
First concert performance Julian Bream/Melos Ensemble/Malcolm Arnold – Jubilee Hall,
  Aldeburgh, 25 June 1959 (Aldeburgh Festival)
First London performance Julian Bream/Melos Ensemble/Malcolm Arnold – Victoria & Albert
  Museum, London, 6 March 1960
First televised performance (Excerpt) Julian Bream/Philharmonia Orchestra/Malcolm Arnold
  – BBC Television, 10 December 1963 ('Gala Performance' series)
First televised performance (complete) Julian Bream/BBC Concert Orchestra/Barry
  Wordsworth – BBC Television, 20 July 1991 (Promenade Concert from the Royal Albert
  Hall, London)
Publisher Paterson, 1961 (also arranged for guitar and piano); Novello, 2006
Articles (i) Classic CD 'Guitar Concerto – Bream at 60' – *Beckus* 9, July 1993; *Maestro* 1,
  October 2014
(ii) Piers Burton-Page, 'Malcolm Arnold and Julian Bream' – *Maestro* 7, October 2020

Kingston Fanfare for brass (1959)
Duration 0'30"
Instrumentation 3 Tpt. 3 Tbn.
Publisher Studio Music, 1986 (as No.1 of 'Four Fanfares')

Sweeney Todd: Ballet Op.68 (1959)
Written for the Royal Ballet Company
Duration 23'
Instrumentation 1+picc./1/2/1 – 2/2/2/0 – timp. perc. pno. cel. hp. str.
First performance Royal Ballet/John Lanchberry – Shakespeare Memorial Theatre, Stratford
  upon-Avon, 10 December 1959

Catalogue of works

Choreography: John Cranko
Designer Alix Stone
Principals: Donald Britton, Elizabeth Anderton, Desmond Doyle, Margaret Knoesen and
Juliaai Musavdal
First London performance above artists, Orchestra of the Royal Opera House, Covent
Garden/Emanuel Young – 16 August 1960
Publisher Faber, 1984
Articles (i) Paul Jackson 'Arnold's Happiest Collaboration' – *Beckus* 24, Spring 1997; *Maestro*
1, October 2014
(ii) Tony Meredith, 'A Sweeney Todd narration' – *Beckus* 119, Winter 2020
(iii) Alan Poulton: 'Sweeney Todd', reviews of the first performance – *Beckus* 119, Winter
2020

(a) Sweeney Todd: Concert Suite Op.68a (1984) arranged by David Ellis
Duration 20'
First performance Bristol University Chamber Orchestra/Christopher Austin – Bristol
University, 19 June 1990
First London performance BBC Concert Orchestra/Barry Wordsworth – Golder's Green
Hippodrome, 27 March 1991
First broadcast performance BBC Concert Orchestra/Malcolm Arnold – Radio 3, 6 November
1991
First Europe performance Göttingen Symphony Orchestra/Urs-Michael Theus – Göttingen,
Niedersachsen, Germany, 22 November 2012
Publisher Faber, 1989
Notes The Eighth Malcolm Arnold Festival featured a version of the Suite, for narrator
and orchestra, written by Tony Meredith and performed in St Matthew's Church,
Northampton, on 19 October 2013, by John Griff (narrator) and the Ealing Symphony
Orchestra conducted by John Gibbons.

(b) Suite from the above arranged for brass band by Phillip Littlemore (2006)
Duration 8'
First performance Rushden Windmill Band/Richard Graves – Royal & Derngate,
Northampton, 22 October 2006 (First Malcolm Arnold Festival)
First Europe performance
Publisher Faber

**(c) Excerpt 'Policeman's Dance' arranged for clarinet and piano by Emma Johnson and
Paul Harris**
Publisher Faber, in 'Concert Repertoire for Clarinet')

(d) Excerpt 'Theme' arranged for flute and piano by Paul Harris
Publisher Trinity/Faber, in 'All Sorts Flute Grades 1-3'

(e) Excerpt 'Theme' arranged for trumpet and piano by John Miller
Publisher Faber, in 'Trumpet Basics'

Song of Simeon: Nativity Masque for mimers, soloists, SATB chorus and orchestra Op.69 (1959)

[Words: Christopher Hassall – 1. Prelude, 2. The Place of the Annunciation, 3. The Inn at Bethlehem, 4. Susana's Dance, 5. Shepherd's Song, 6. Arak's Scene, 7. Processional Hymn, 8. Outside the Temple]
Written for a charity matinee in aid of refugee children*
Duration 29'30"
Instrumentation 0/0/0/0 – 0/3/3/1 – timp. perc.(2) cel. hp. str.
Alt instrumentation Recorders, piano duet, timp. perc. str.
First performance Nicholas Chagrin/Imogen Hassall/St Martin's Singers and Concert Orchestra/Malcolm Arnold – Drury Lane Theatre, London, 5 January 1960 (concert given under the auspices of the Vicar of St Martin-in-the-Fields)
    Producer: Colin Graham
    Choreography: John Cranko
    Designer: Annena Stubbs
First broadcast performance Ambrosian Singers/English Chamber Orchestra/Malcolm Arnold – Radio 3, 12 January 1967 (from Walthamstow Town Hall)
    Principals: Ann Dowdall, Christopher Keyte, Forbes Robinson, Jean Allister and Ian Partridge (in the title role)
Notes (i) *'Song of Simeon' was given a second performance on 19 December 1960 and in the presence of Queen Elizabeth the Queen Mother. This was the third of the St Martin-in-the-Fields charity matinees and was in aid of the 'Save the Children Fund' – the conductor on this occasion was not Malcolm Arnold but John Churchill.
(ii) The masque has not received many foreign performances but there was one in Japan on 20 February 2000 performed by the Misawa Shogyo High School Chorus and Orchestra at the Misawa City Auditorium.
Publisher OUP, 1960; Faber, 1987 (vocal score)

(a) Excerpt 'The Pilgrim Caravan' arranged for unaccompanied SATB chorus
Duration 3'
Publisher OUP, 1960; Faber, 1986

(b) Excerpt 'The Pilgrim Caravan' arranged for unison voices (with optional descant) and orchestra
Instrumentation 2/2/2/2 – 2/3/3/0 – timp. perc.(2) pno. str.
Alt instrumentation pno. str.
Publisher OUP, 1960; Faber, 1986

(c) Excerpt 'The Pilgrim Caravan' arranged for unaccompanied unison voices
Publisher Faber 1987

(d) Excerpt 'The Pilgrim Caravan' arranged for SATB chorus and piano
Publisher Faber, 1987

Parasol: BBC musical (1960)

[Book and Lyrics by Caryl Brahms and Ned Sherrin based on the 'Anatol' dialogues by Arthur Schnitzler – 1. 'Only a Parasol', 2. 'The Face of Love', 3. 'A Woman would be lost without a Man', 4. 'Goodbye Champagne', 5. 'Sleep', 6. 'Who do I Love?', 7. 'The Other One', 8. 'Don't think it hasn't been fun']

Commissioned for BBC Television by Eric Maschwitz, Head of Television Light Entertainment
Duration 75'
Music played by: Eric Robinson Orchestra/Marcus Dods
Musical numbers staged by: Alfred Rodrigues
First broadcast performance BBC Television, 20 March 1960 (pre-recorded 18 March 1960)
  Producer: Ned Sherrin
  Designer: Clifford Hatts
  Costumes: Angela Flanders
  Principals: William Hutt (as Anatol), Hy Hazell (Ilona), Pip Hinton (Anna Louise), Peter
  Sallis (Max), Irene Hamilton (Gabrielle), Moira Redmond (Lulu)
First staged performance pupils of Wymondham College/Orchestra/Ian Hytch – Sports
  Hall, Wymondham College, Norfolk, 8-10 May 1987 (three performances which were
  broadcast by Radio Norfolk – Producer: Stewart Orr)
  Designer: David Chedgy
  Choreography: Beverley Wedgwood
Publisher Feldman, 1961 (vocal selections)
Notes The rehearsals and performance were filmed by BBC Television, with both Ned
  Sherrin and Malcolm Arnold in attendance
Articles (i) Janine Hytch, 'Wymondham Symphony Orchestra' – *Beckus* 20, Spring 1996;
  Maestro 1, October 2014
(ii) Alan Poulton, 'Parasol' – *Beckus* 104, Spring 2017
(iii) Piers Burton-Page, 'More on 'Parasol'' – *Beckus* 105, Summer 2017
(iv) Ian Hytch, 'Reviving 'Parasol'' – *Beckus* 106, Autumn 2017

**(a) A Pride of Parasols for choir and orchestra (2017) excerpts arranged into a suite of
songs by Ian Hytch**
Duration 20'
First performance Framlingham Earl Singers/Orchestra/Ian Hytch – Central Baptist Church,
  Norwich, 6 May 2017*
Notes *Almost thirty years to the day when Ian Hytch conducted the world stage premiere
  of 'Parasol' at Wymondham College.
Article Jenny Newton, 'A Pride of Parasols' – *Beckus* 106, Autumn 2017

Fantasy for flute and guitar (1960)
Written for Katherine and Robert Arnold to play together
Duration 1'30"
First concert performance Flautist (un-named)/Milos Karadaglic (Gtr.) – Royal & Derngate,
  Northampton, 19 October 2008 (Third Malcolm Arnold Festival)
Publisher QTP

(a) arranged for flute and clarinet by Paul Harris (2006)
First concert performance Eleanor Blamires (Fl.)/Caitlin McErlean (Cl.) – Royal & Derngate,
  Northampton, 21 October 2006 (First Malcolm Arnold Festival)
Publisher QTP

March: 'Overseas' for military band Op.70 (1960)
Commissioned by the Central Office of Information for the 1960 British Trade Fair in New
  York

Duration 2'30"
First performance New York, January 1960
Publisher Novello/Paterson; Carl Fischer (New York), 1960

(a) arranged for brass band by Neil Richmond (2008)
First performance Rushden Windmill Band/Martin Dummer – Royal & Derngate,
    Northampton, 22 October 2012 (Seventh Malcolm Arnold Festival)
Unpublished

Symphony No.4 Op.71 (1960)
Commissioned by the BBC
Duration 36'
Instrumentation 2+picc./2/2/2 + cbsn. – 4/3/3/1 – timp. perc.(3) cel. hp. str.
First performance BBC Symphony Orchestra/Malcolm Arnold – Royal Festival Hall, London, 2
    November 1960
First broadcast performance above artists – Home Service, 11 November 1960 (repeated on
    the Third Programme, 12 November 1960
First Australia performance Fremantle Symphony Orchestra – Fremantle Town Hall, 15
    September 2002
First US performance Willimantic Orchestra – Coventry, CT, 9 November 2003
Publisher Paterson, 1960
Articles (i) John Gibbons, 'The Fourth Symphony' – *Beckus* 74, Autumn 2009
(ii) Kevin Oxlade: 'Havant Symphony Orchestra' (Symphony No.4) – *Beckus* 85, Summer
    2012
(iii) David Dunstan, 'The mystery of the Fourth Symphony' – *Beckus* 93, Summer 2014
(iv) Piers Burton-Page, 'A small part of the work? The Fourth Symphony revisited' – *Beckus*
    118, Autumn 2020
(v) David Dunstan, 'Thoughts on the Fourth Symphony' (with music examples) – *Maestro* 7,
    October 2020

(a) arranged for wind band by Munetoshi Senoo (2007)
Duration 18'30"
First performance Bunkyo University Wind Orchestra/Munetoshi Senoo – Tokyo, 2007
Notes A very truncated version of the symphony

Carnival of Animals for orchestra Op.72 (1960)
[1. The Giraffe 2. Sheep 3. Cows 4. Mice 5. Jumbo* 6. Chiroptera (Bats)]
Commissioned for the Hoffnung Memorial Concert
Duration 8'30"
Instrumentation 2+picc./2/2/2 – 4/3/3/1 – timp. perc.(2) str.
First performance Morley College Symphony Orchestra/Malcolm Arnold – Royal Festival
    Hall, London, 31 October 1960 (Hoffnung Memorial Concert)
First Japan performance Tokyo Symphony Orchestra – Yamanashi Prefectural Hall, Kofu, 2
    August 1996 (and repeated in Tokyo on 3 August)
First US performance Austin Symphony Orchestra/Peter Bay – Bass Concert Hall, Austin,
    Texas – 14 March 2003 (and repeated the following day)
First Europe performance Bruckner Orchestra/Max Renne – Brucknerhaus, Linz, Austria, 8
    April 2003

Catalogue of works

Publisher Novello
Notes "Here the composer 'borrows' the famous pizzicato movement from Sylvia by Delibes!

A Hoffnung Fanfare (1960)
Written for the Hoffnung Memorial Concert
Duration 2'
Instrumentation 36 trumpets in 3 groups of 12 – side drum, bass drum and timpani
First performance Trumpeters of the Royal Military School of Music, Kneller Hall – Royal Festival Hall, London, 31 October 1960 (Hoffnung Memorial Concert)
First modern performance 'Festival Brass'/Ben Hoffnung – Royal & Derngate, Northampton – 17 October 2015 (Tenth Malcolm Arnold Festival)
Publisher Triplo, 1981

(a) arranged for 12 trumpets by James Olcott (1981)
Publisher Triplo, 1981

Brass Quintet No.1 Op.73 (1961)
Written for and dedicated to the New York Brass Quintet
Duration 13'
Instrumentation Tpt.(2) Hn. Tbn. Tba.
First performance New York Brass Quintet* – New York, 1961
First UK performance Francis Chagrin Ensemble – London, 17 March 1962 (St Pancras Festival)
First broadcast performance New Brass Consort of Manchester – Northern Home Service, 4 January 1963 (from Milton Hall, Manchester)
Publisher Paterson, 1961
Notes (i) *The Quintet toured the UK in August 1965 and recorded two movements from Arnold's Brass Quintet for BBC 2 Television in the series 'Music on Two'; their performance was televised on 17 January 1966
(ii) An excerpt from the Brass Quintet was used as the theme music for the BBC Television series 'Election Forum' and presented by Ludovic Kennedy in advance of the General Election held on 10 October 1974.

Fanfare for the Farnham Festival (1961)
Written for the inaugural Farnham Festival (the composer's gift)
Duration c.2'
Instrumentation 5Hn. 6Tpt. 5Tbn. Tba. Cym. Timp.
First performance Brass of Tiffin School, Kingston upon Thames and Farnham Grammar School/Denis Bloodworth – Farnham Parish Church, Farnham, Surrey, 8 May 1961 (Farnham Festival)
Publisher QTP

arranged for string orchestra by Jonathan Whiting (2018)
First performance Malcolm Arnold Festival Orchestra/Hilary Davan Wetton – Malcolm Arnold Academy, Northampton, 13 October 2018 (Thirteenth Malcolm Arnold Festival)

Symphony No.5 Op.74 (1961)

Commissioned by the Cheltenham Festival Society
Duration 33'
Instrumentation 2+picc./2/2/2 – 4/3/3/1 – timp. perc.(2) cel. hp. str.
First performance Hallé Orchestra/Malcolm Arnold – Cheltenham Town Hall, 3 July 1961
  (Cheltenham Festival)
First broadcast performance BBC Northern Symphony Orchestra/Malcolm Arnold – BBC
  Music Programme, 1 May 1967 (recorded 26 January 1966 in 'The British Symphony'
  series, and repeated on 28 June 1968)
First London performance New Philharmonia Orchestra/Malcolm Arnold – Royal Festival
  Hall, London, 16 December 1971
First Europe performance Manchester Youth Orchestra – Église Saint-Médard de Thouars,
  France, 29 July 1984
First US performance University of Arizona Symphony Orchestra – Tucson, Arizona, 19 April
  1998
First Japan performance Tokyo University Student Orchestra/James Lockhart – Tokyo
  University, 2 July 1999
First Russia performance St Petersburg State Academy Orchestra/Rudi Eastwood –
  Beloselsky-Belozersky Palace, St Petersburg, 31 October 2007 (British Music Festival)
Publisher Paterson, 1961; Novello, 2000
Notes The composer comments in a programme note that "After the first performance of
  my Fourth Symphony there were so many things I felt needed to be said musically that I
  am more than grateful for the opportunity given me by the Cheltenham Festival Society
  to attempt to say these things."
Articles (i) Sheldon Bair, 'Fifth Symphony in Bel Air' – *Beckus* 92, Spring 2014
(ii) R.V.W. review of the Fifth Symphony: 'Black mark for putting a tune into a symphony',
  from the *Richmond and Twickenham Times*, 8 July 1961 – *Beckus* 103, Winter 2016

**(a) Two Symphonic Movements Op.74a (2000) arranged for wind band by Munetoshi
  Senoo and Bram Gay**
First performance Bunkyo University Wind Orchestra/Munetoshi Senoo – Tokyo, 2000
First UK performance Manchester University Wind Orchestra – Royal Northern College of
  Music, Manchester, 28 April 2000
Publisher Studio Music
Notes Movements 2 and 4 of Symphony No.5 Op.74

(b) Excerpt 'Slow Movement Theme' arranged for piano solo by Stephen Duro
Publisher Chester Music/Music Sales Ltd, 1997 (in 'Contemporary Classics' No.2)

[as a ballet] Generation Y: Ballet (2016)
First performance Oldenburg Ballet Company – Oldenburg State Theatre, Germany, 5 March
  2016
Choreography: Antoine Jully
Article 'Generation Y in Oldenburg', *Beckus* 102, Autumn 2016

Divertimento No.2 for orchestra Op.75 (1961)

[1. Fanfare 2. Nocturne 3. Chaconne]
Duration 9'
Instrumentation 2+picc./2/2/2 – 4/3/3/1 – timp. perc.(2) hp. str.

First performance Royal Liverpool Philharmonic Orchestra/Lawrence Leonard – Leeds Town Hall, 24 October 1961 (Rostrum Concert – repeated in Preston on 25 October and Liverpool, 26 October)

First London performance Royal Philharmonic Orchestra/Kenneth V Jones – Royal Festival Hall, London, 26 March 1962

Publisher Paterson, 1961

Notes This is a re-orchestration of the 1950 Divertimento No.2 and a change of central movement title from the original 'Tango' to 'Nocturne'

Article Alan Poulton, '... the mystery of Divertimento No.2' – *Maestro* 2, October 2015

Grand Concerto Gastronomique for eater, waiter, food and large orchestra Op.76 (1961)

[1. Prologue – Oysters, 2. Soup – Brown Windsor, 3. Roast Beef, 4. Cheese, 5. Peach Melba, 6. Coffee, Brandy, Epilogue]

Written for the Hoffnung Astronautical Music Festival

Duration 20'

Instrumentation 2+picc./2/2/2 – 4/3/3/1 – timp. perc.(2) hp. str.

First performance Henry Sherek (eater)/Tutte Lemkow (waiter)/Morley College Symphony Orchestra/Malcolm Arnold – Royal Festival Hall, London, 28 November 1961 (Hoffnung Astronautical Music Festival)

First modern performance Richard Brooman (eater)/Martha Shrimpton (waiter)/Ealing Symphony Orchestra/John Gibbons – Royal & Derngate, Northampton, 22 October 2011 (Sixth Malcolm Arnold Festival)

Unpublished

Leonora No.4 (Beethoven-Strasser) Overture for large orchestra (1961)

Written for the Hoffnung Astronautical Music Festival

Duration 9'30"

Instrumentation 2+picc./2/2/2 – 4/2/3/1 – timp. perc.(2) str. (+ off-stage trumpets and street band)

First performance Morley College Symphony Orchestra/Norman Del Mar – Royal Festival Hall, London, 28 November 1961 (Hoffnung Astronautical Music Festival)

Unpublished

Concerto for two violins and string orchestra Op.77 (1962)

Written for Yehudi Menuhin and his pupil Alberto Lysy

Duration 16'30"

First performance Yehudi Menuhin/Alberto Lysy/Bath Festival Orchestra/Malcolm Arnold – Bath Guildhall, 24 June 1962 (Bath Festival)

First London performance Yehudi Menuhin/Robert Masters/Bath Festival Orchestra/Malcolm Arnold – Victoria & Albert Museum, London, 17 June 1964

First broadcast performance Alfredo Campoli/Derek Collier/London Symphony Orchestra/Malcolm Arnold – BBC Music Programme, 28 December 1965 (recorded 26 September in the 'Composer's Portrait' series)

First US performance Paul King/Peter McHugh/Louisville Orchestra/Jorge Mester – Louisville, Kentucky, c.1974 (and subsequently recorded on the Louisville label)

Publisher Faber, 1966 (also arranged for violin and piano by Elspeth Roseberry)

Notes The score was begun in India while the composer was working on his researches for the film score 'Nine Hours to Rama'.

Little Suite No.2 for orchestra Op.78 (1962)
[1. Overture 2. Ballad 3. Dance]
Commissioned by Elphicks of Farnham for the 1963 Farnham Festival
Duration 10'
Instrumentation 2/2/2/2 – 4/3/3/1 – timp. perc.(3) str.
First performance Combined Orchestras of Farnham Grammar School and Tiffin School, Kingston upon Thames/Denis Bloodworth – Farnham Parish Church, Surrey, 13 May 1963 (Farnham Festival)
First London performance London Junior and Senior Orchestras/Oliver Broome – Royal Festival Hall, London, 25 May 1964
First broadcast performance BBC Northern Ireland Orchestra/Terence Lovett – Network Three, 30 September 1965
Publisher Paterson, 1963
Article Fiona Southey, 'If at First You Don't Succeed' – *Beckus* 32, Spring 99; *Maestro* 1, October 2014 – the story of the Music for Youth Orchestra, who beat the Guinness World Record for the World's Largest Orchestra: 3,503 players were conducted by Simon Rattle in the National Indoor Arena in Birmingham on 23 November 1998 and in the presence of the composer. (The previous record was 2,212 players by Kent Music Schools.)

(a) Attleborough Suite for brass band Op.78a (2000) arranged by Bram Gay
First concert performance Ipswich and Norwich Band/Robin Norman – Royal & Derngate, Northampton, 25 October 2009 (Fourth Malcolm Arnold Festival)
Publisher Studio Music

(b) Attleborough Suite for wind band Op.78b (2000) arranged by Denis Bloodworth
Publisher Novello

(c) arranged for recorder orchestra by Denis Bloodworth (with Little Suite No.1 Op.53)
First performance London Recorder Orchestra/Denis Bloodworth – summer concert, 1996
Unpublished

The Peacock in the Zoo: song for voice and piano (1963)
[Words: Katherine Arnold*]
Duration 2'
First performance Claire Thompson (Sop.)/Scott Mitchell (Pno.) – Royal & Derngate, Northampton, 20 October 2013 (Eighth Malcolm Arnold Festival)
Publisher Paterson, 1963; QTP
Notes *The composer's daughter and eldest of his three children, see also Symphony No.7 Op.113.

Elektra: Ballet in one act Op.79 (1963)
Commissioned by the Royal Ballet Company
Duration 25'
Instrumentation 2+picc./2/2/2 – 4/3/3/1 – timp. perc.(3) hp. str.

First performance Royal Ballet/John Lanchberry – Royal Opera House, Covent Garden,
London, 26 March 1963
Choreography: Robert Helpmann
Decor: Arthur Boyd
Principals: Nadia Nerina, David Blair, Monica Mason, Derek Rencher
First Australia performance Australian Ballet Company – Adelaide, 14 March 1966
Article Paul Jackson, 'A Portrait of Obsessive Revenge' – *Beckus* 25, Summer 1997; *Maestro*
1, October 2014

(a) Elektra: Ballet Suite Op.79a (2004) arranged by David Ellis
Duration 15'
First concert performance BBC Concert Orchestra/Barry Wordsworth – Royal Festival Hall,
London, 5 November 2004 (a Gala Concert given in partnership with the Association of
British Orchestras and broadcast 'live' on Radio 3)
Publisher Novello

Espionage: ATV series (1963)
[Arnold contributed music to 14 episodes* (of 24) plus the opening and closing titles as
follows: 1. 'The Weakling', 2. 'A Covenant with Death', 3. 'He Rises on Sunday and We
on Monday', 4. 'The Gentle Spy', 5. 'The Dragon Slayer', 6. 'To the Very End', 7. 'A Camel
to Ride, a Sheep to Eat', 8. 'The Light of a Friendly Star', 9. 'A Tiny Drop of Poison', 10.
'Festival of Pawns', 11. 'Never Turn your Back on a Friend', 12. 'Medal for a Turned Coat',
13. 'Sentence of Death', 14. 'Do You Remember Leo Winters?']
Executive Producer: Herbert Hirschman
Music conducted by: Malcolm Arnold
Notes *The first episode was transmitted by ITV on 5 October 1963 (UK); NBC, 1963-64 (US);
Tokyo Broadcasting System, 1966 (Japan)

Gala Performance: signature tune for BBC Television series (1963)
Duration 1'30
Instrumentation 2/2/2/2 – 4/2/3/1 – timp. perc.(2) hp. gtr. str.
First broadcast performance – BBC Television, 19 November 1963 (pre-recorded 27 October
1963)
Music played by: Eric Robinson Orchestra/Malcolm Arnold
Producer: Patricia Foy
Designer: Clifford Hatts
Presenter: Richard Attenborough
Notes A revised version of the opening and closing titles was recorded on 2 October 1964
and transmitted for the first time on 23 October 1964

Little Suite No.1 for brass band Op.80 (1963)
[1. Prelude 2. Siciliano 3. Rondo]
Commissioned by the Scottish Amateur Music Association for the National Youth Brass
Band of Scotland
Duration 10'
First performance National Youth Brass Band of Scotland/Bryden Thomson – Aberdeen High
School for Girls, July 1963
First broadcast performance Hanwell Brass Band/Eric Bravington – 30 November 1965

Publisher Paterson, 1965; Studio Music

(a) arranged for symphonic wind band by John Paynter (1964)
First Europe performance Ulm Symphonic Wind Orchestra/Douglas Bostock – Ulm, Germany, 12 May 2001
Publisher Novello/Paterson; Carl Fischer (New York) (as 'Prelude, Siciliano and Rondo Op.80a')

(b) arranged for wind band by Hans Moeckel (1971)
Publisher Emil Ruh

(c) arranged for military band by Denis Bloodworth
Publisher Molenaar (Netherlands)

(d) arranged for orchestra by Philip Lane (1999)
Instrumentation 2/2/2/2 – 4/3/3/0 – timp.perc.(2) str
First performance Charterhouse School Orchestra/Robin Wells – Godalming, Surrey, 23 November 2001
Publisher Novello, as Little Suite No.4 for orchestra Op.80a (1999)

Sinfonietta No.3 for chamber orchestra Op.81 (1964)
Duration 14'30"
Instrumentation 1/2/0/2 – 2/0/0/0 – str.
First performance New Philharmonia Orchestra/Malcolm Arnold – Fairfield Hall, Croydon, Surrey, 30 January 1965
First broadcast performance BBC Concert Orchestra/Malcolm Arnold – Radio 3, BBC Music Programme, 10 October 1967 (Midday Concert recorded 5 October 1967)
Publisher Paterson, 1964
Article Piers Burton-Page, 'Three's Company: the Sinfoniettas' – *Beckus* 98, Autumn 2015

Water Music for wind and percussion Op.82 (1964)
Commissioned by the National Trust in celebration of the opening of the Stratford Canal.
Duration 10'
Instrumentation 2+picc./2/2 + EbCl./2/ – 4/3/3/1 – perc.(2)
First performance Ensemble/Brian Priestman – Stratford-upon-Avon, 11 July 1964 (after a performance of Shakespeare's 'Henry V')*
First concert performance Royal Northern College of Music Wind Ensemble/Clark Rundell – Royal Northern College of Music, Manchester, 3 November 1984 (BASWBE Conference)
Publisher Studio Music
Notes *Played by musicians on a barge moored in the middle of the River Avon at the point where the Stratford Canal enters the river behind the Shakespeare Memorial Theatre. The composer was made a life member of the Trust soon afterwards.

(a) Water Music for orchestra Op.82a (1964) arrangement
Instrumentation 2+picc./2/2/2 – 4/3/3/1 – timp. perc.(2) str.
First performance Hallé Orchestra/Lawrence Leonard – Free Trade Hall, Manchester, 21 March 1965
First Europe performance Munich Symphony Orchestra/Douglas Bostock – Klosterhof Reichenau, Germany, 20-22 June 2001 (three performances)

Catalogue of works

First broadcast performance BBC Symphony Orchestra/Michael Collins – recorded in Maida
    Vale Studios, London, 6 January 2016
First Japan performance Tokyo Philharmonic Orchestra/Yuto Suzuki – NHK Hall, Tokyo, 13
    October 2016
First US performance Susquehanna Symphony Orchestra/Sheldon Bair – Bel Air, Maryland,
    14 October 2017
First London performance South East London Orchestra/David Smith – St Barnabas Church,
    Beckenham, 3 December 2017
Publisher Paterson, 1965

A Sunshine Overture for orchestra Op.83 (1964)
Written at the request of Beryl Grey for a Gala matinee in aid of the Sunshine Home for
    Blind Babies
Duration 2'
Instrumentation 2/2/2/2 – 2/2/1/0 – perc. str.
First performance Sunshine Gala Orchestra (a.k.a. the Pro Arte Orchestra)/Dudley Simpson –
    Palace Theatre, London, 14 July 1964*
Article Alan Poulton, 'The Sunshine Matinees' – Beckus 97, Summer 2015
Notes *The Overture was also played at the following year's Gala matinee, held at the
    Theatre Royal, Drury Lane, on 13 July 1965 again conducted by Dudley Simpson – after
    that, the score appears to have disappeared and may be regarded as lost. See Beckus
    107, Winter 2017 for a full list of other Arnold 'missing scores'.

Five Pieces for violin and piano Op.84 (1964)
[1. Prelude, 2. Aubade (based on an Indian raga), 3. Waltz, 4. Ballad (derived from the Arioso
    in the ballet Rinaldo and Armida q.v.), 5. Moto perpetuo (dedicated to Charlie Parker)]
Written for Yehudi Menuhin to use on his American tour as 'encore' pieces
Duration 9'
First performance Yehudi Menuhin (Vn.)/Ivor Newton (Pno.) – Bamburgh Castle,
    Northumberland, 24 July 1965
First broadcast performance Derek Collier (Vn.)/Ernest Lush (Pno.) – Home Service, 29
    January 1966
First Canada performance Ruggiero Ricci (Vn.)/Rebecca Pennies (Pno.) – Victoria, British
    Columbia, July/August 1970 (played at sight and in the presence of the composer)*
First Europe performance Gerd Jansen – Germany, 5 June 2004
Notes *This performance was recorded and later issued on a CD entitled 'Ricci in Concert
    Vol. 3' in 1991
Publisher Paterson, 1965
Article Peter Fisher, 'Five Pieces for violin and piano in Italy' – Beckus 112, Spring 2019

(a) arranged for violin and string orchestra by Philip Lane (2005)
First performance Chamber Orchestra of Lapland/John Storgårds – Ivalo, Finland, 23
    February 2007
First UK performance Sinfonia Viva/Benedict Holland – Drill Hall, Lincoln, 9 March 2014
First London performance Chamber Ensemble of London/Peter Fisher – St James's,
    Piccadilly, 14 May 2016
Publisher Novello, 2005 (as Op.84a)
Article Alan Poulton, 'Works for soloists and strings' – Beckus 101, Summer 2016

Duo for two cellos Op.85 (1965)
Commissioned by Novello for a teaching book
Duration 5'
Publisher Novello, 1971 (in 'Playing the Cello' by Hugo Cole and Anna Shuttleworth)

also arranged for two violas by Alison Milne
Publisher Novello, 1986

Theme for 'Players' (1965)
Written for John Player Tobacco as an TV advertising theme – it was not used.
Duration 45"

(a) Thême pour mon Amis (1984) revised and arranged for whistler and piano by Alan Poulton (at the request of the composer)
Commissioned by John Amis for performance on the BBC Television programme 'My Music'
Duration 70"
First performance John Amis (whistler)/Steve Race (Pno.) – BBC 2 Television, 19 December
1985 ('My Music' Christmas Programme)

(b) Solitaire for flute and piano (2003) [arrangement]
First performance Claire Fillhart (Fl)/Claire Dunham (Pno.) – Royal & Derngate,
Northampton, 7 October 2007 (Second Malcolm Arnold Festival)
Publisher QTP

(c) arranged for recorder and string quartet as 'Whistling Tune'
First performance Jill Kemp (Rec.)/Arran Quartet – Royal & Derngate, Northampton, 25
October 2009 (Fourth Malcolm Arnold Festival)

Fantasies for solo wind instruments
Arnold was commissioned by the City of Birmingham Symphony Orchestra to write a series of five solo Fantasies for the Birmingham International Wind Competition in 1966.
Article: Alan Poulton, 'Birmingham International Wind competition 1966', Maestro 2, October 2015

Fantasy for bassoon Op.86 (1965)
Duration 4'30"
First performance John Mostard – Birmingham Town Hall, 17 May 1966
First broadcast performance Joanna Graham – Scottish Home Service (from Glasgow), 1
September 1968 (recorded 23 August 1968)
Publisher Faber, 1966
Notes The class winner was Frantisek Herman (Czechoslovakia)
Article Laurence Perkins, 'Fantasy for bassoon' (with music examples) – *Maestro* 4, October
2017

Fantasy for clarinet Op.87 (1966)
Duration 4'30"
First performance Edward Godsell – Birmingham Town Hall, 18 May 1966

Catalogue of works

Publisher Faber, 1966
Notes The class winner was Aurelian-Octav Popa (Romania) who also won the Open Second
    Prize.
Article Janet Hilton, 'Playing Malcolm's clarinet works' – Beckus 101, Summer 2016

Fantasy for horn Op.88 (1966)
Duration 4'30"
First performance James Diack* – Birmingham Town Hall, 22 May 1966
First broadcast performance Alan Civil – Radio 3, BBC Music Programme, 11 October 1967
Publisher Faber, 1966
Notes (i) The class winner was Ferenc Tarjani (Hungary).
(ii) *Son of Michael Diack, who was Arnold's publisher at Paterson's during the fifties.
Article (i) Frank Lloyd, 'Fantasy for horn Op.88' (with music examples) – Maestro 3, October
    2016

Fantasy for flute Op.89 (1966)
Duration 4'30"
First performance Per Oien – Birmingham Town Hall, 19 May 1966
First London performance Elizabeth Dean – Bethnal Green, 1967 (Society for Modern Music
    Concert)
Publisher Faber, 1966
Notes The class winner was James Galway who also shared the Open First Prize with
    Maurice Bourgue
Article Carl Willetts 'A Morning off School' – Beckus 98, Autumn 2015

Fantasy for oboe Op.90 (1966)
Duration 4'30"
First performance Maurice Bourgue – Birmingham Town Hall, 20 May 1966
Publisher Faber, 1966
Notes The class winner was Maurice Bourgue (France) and, despite the pressure of being
    the first of the 23 competitors to perform, he played the Fantasy from memory.
    Bourgue also shared the Open First Prize with James Galway.
Article Sarah Roper, 'Fantasy for oboe, Op.90' (with music examples) – Maestro 4,
    October 2017

Four Cornish Dances for orchestra Op.91 (1966)
Dedicated to the composer's second wife, Isobel
Duration 10'
Instrumentation 2+picc./2/2/2 – 4/3/3/1 – timp. perc.(2) hp. str.
First performance London Philharmonic Orchestra/Malcolm Arnold – Royal Albert Hall,
    London, 13 August 1966 (Promenade Concert broadcast 'live' on the Home Service)
First US performance Pittsburgh Symphony Orchestra – Pittsburgh, 16 October 1981
First Europe broadcast performance Norwegian Broadcasting Orchestra – Radio Norway,
    Oslo, 24 January 1982
First Europe concert performance RTE Concert Orchestra – National Concert Hall, Dublin, 17
    April 1983
First South Africa performance Cape Town Symphony Orchestra – Cape Town, 16 March 1986

57

First New Zealand performance Hampshire County Youth Orchestra/Edgar Holmes – Napier Boys' High School, 2 August 1993
First Canada performance Brantford Symphony Orchestra/Stanley Saunders – Brantford, Ontario, 24 April 1994
First Australia performance Western Australian Youth Orchestra/John Iverson – Perth, 18 May 1996
First Asia performance Malaysian Philharmonic Orchestra/Kees Bakels – Petronas Philharmonic Hall, Kuala Lumpur, Malaysia, 14 September 1998
First Japan performance Festine-Lente Ensemble/Taizo Takemoto – Life Port, Toyohashi, 5 August 2001
Publisher Faber, 1968
Notes Dance No.1 was used in Series 2 No.3 of the BBC Television programme 'Roots of England', presented by Brian Trueman and transmitted between September 1980 and March 1981. It was also used as the theme music for the BBC (Bristol) Television series 'Rick Stein's Taste of the Sea' first transmitted on BBC 2 Television, 12 September 1995.

(a) arranged by the composer with additional parts for brass band (1968)
First performance Penzance Orchestral Society/Cornwall Symphony Orchestra/St Dennis Silver Band/St Agnes Silver Band/Malcolm Arnold – Truro Cathedral, Cornwall, 16 March 1968

(b) arranged for wind band by Thad Marciniak (1968)
Publisher Faber, 1968 and G. Schirmer (New York), 1975

(c) arranged for brass band by Ray Farr (1985)
First performance Royal Marines Band – Deal, Kent, 5 October 1989
First London performance Williams Fairey Band/Yorkshire Imperial Band/Geoffrey Brand – Kenwood House, London, 28 April 1996
Publisher Faber, 1985

(d) arranged for wind, percussion and harp by Ruth Thorpe (1995)
Instrumentation 2fl.+ picc. 2 ob. 4cl.+bcl. 2 al.sax. 2 bsn. – timp. perc.(2) str.
First performance Wakefield Metropolitan Youth Wind Orchestra/Philip Wood – Wakefield Cathedral, 30 June 1995
Publisher Da Capo, 1995

(e) Dance Nos. 1 and 3 arranged for recorder ensemble by Denis Bloodworth (1997)
Publisher Faber, 1997

(f) Dance No.1 arranged for piano solo by Cecil Bolton (1968)
Publisher Chester, 1968 (as 'Roots of England' TV theme)

(g) Dance No.1 arranged for clarinet and piano by Paul Harris
Publisher Trinity/Faber, in 'All Sorts Clarinet Grades 1-3'

(h) Dance No.1 arranged for trumpet and piano by John Miller
Publisher Faber, in 'Trumpet Basics'

Theme and Variation: for Severn Bridge Variations on a Welsh Folk Song 'Braint' for orchestra: composite work (1966)

Written to commemorate the first birthday of the BBC Training Orchestra on its first visit to Wales and of the opening of the first Severn Bridge.
Duration 19'30" (complete work)
Instrumentation 3/2+ca./2+bcl./o – 4/3/3/1 – timp. perc.(2) hp. str.
First performance BBC Training Orchestra/Sir Adrian Boult – Brangwyn Hall, Swansea, 11 January 1967 (and broadcast 'live' on the Home Service)
First London performance BBC Welsh Symphony Orchestra/Boris Brott – Royal Albert Hall, London, 20 July 1976 (Promenade Concert)
Notes The other contributors were Alun Hoddinott, Nicholas Maw, Daniel Jones, Grace Williams and Michael Tippett, an equitable split of three Welsh and three English composers!
Unpublished

The Shipwright's Song: for unison voices (1966)

[Words: Bill Musitano*]
Duration 2'
First public performance (arranged by Alan Poulton) An 'ad hoc' group led by Alison Harvey (Sop.) and Hannah Hawken (Cnt.) – The Shipwrights, Padstow Harbour, Cornwall, 26 May 2014 (after the unveiling of a special memorial plaque donated by Frank Brand)
Notes *Bill was the landlord of The Shipwrights during the 1960s and knew Malcolm well; his son, Chris, had sent the song from Ireland where he now lives.
Article Colin Gregory, 'Scratch choir premieres The Shipwright's Song' – *Beckus* 94, Autumn 2014

Tommy's Titifala: song for unison voices (c.1966)

[Words: Tommy Morrissey]
Written for and probably first performed by Tommy Morrissey, a local fisherman and folk singer – according to Jean Morrissey (then aged 90) back in 2014, the score was "somewhere" at her daughter's house.

Jolly Old Friar, for unison voices and piano (1965)

[Words: Frank Richards]
First performance BBC Radio 3 announcers – Radio 3, 15 March 1991 ('Comic Relief' Night)
First concert performance Claire Thompson (Sop.)/Scott Mitchell (Pno.) – Royal & Derngate, Northampton, 19 October 2014 (Ninth Malcolm Arnold Festival)
Publisher Cassell, 1965 (in 'Greyfriar's School: A Prospectus')

The Turtle Drum: a children's play for television Op.92 (1967)

[Libretto: Ian Serraillier – 1. The Turtle Drum, 2. Go back where you belong (Part 1), 3. Round of Welcome, 4. Divertissement of the Deep, 5. The Four Seasons, 6. Sayonara Song, 7. Go back where you belong (Part 2)]
Commissioned by BBC Television for their opening programme of a series entitled 'Making Music'
Duration 50'
Instrumentation Fl./Picc. Tpt. Gtr.(s) Perc. Db.

First performance James Blades and pupils of the David Livingstone Primary School – BBC
Television, 26 April 1967
Series Producer: John Hosier
Director: Moyra Gambleton
Publisher OUP, 1968; Faber
Notes Originally entitled 'Kaisoo the Fisherboy'
Article Katherine and Kevin Oxlade, 'A Child's View' – *Beckus* 58, Autumn 2005

(a) arranged for children's voices and chamber orchestra by Timothy Bowers* (2019)
Instrumentation 2/0/0/0 – 2/0/0/0 – str.
First performance Malcolm Arnold Academy and Preparatory School students/Alina
Orchestra/Hilary Davan Wetton – Malcolm Arnold Academy, Northampton, 12 October
2019 (Fourteenth Malcolm Arnold Festival)
Notes *Includes additional incidental music – the orchestration is identical to that of the
Sinfonietta No.2 Op.65 which the orchestra had also featured in the concert.

Little Suite No.2 for brass band Op.93 (1967)
[1. Round 2. Cavatina 3. Galop]
Commissioned by the Cornwall Youth Brass Band
Duration 8'45"
First performance Cornwall Youth Brass Band/Malcolm Arnold – Fowey, Cornwall, 26 March
1967
First broadcast performance Brighouse & Rastrick Band/Carlton Main Frickley Colliery
Band/Grimethorpe Colliery Band/Malcolm Arnold – Radio 3, 19 August 1968 (part of a
concert given at the Sheffield City Hall during the 1968 Sheffield Arts Festival)
Publisher Henrees Music, 1967; Studio Music

(a) arranged for military band by Jan Singerling (1967)
Publisher Molenaar (Netherlands), 1967

(b) arranged for large orchestra by Philip Lane (2000)
Instrumentation 2/2/2/2 – 4/3/3/0 – timp. perc.(3) str.
First performance Northampton Symphony Orchestra/John Gibbons – Spinney Hill Theatre,
Northampton, 7 July 2007
Notes The first performance was originally slated for the Second Malcolm Arnold Festival in
October 2007.
Publisher Novello, as Little Suite No.5 for orchestra Op.93a (2000)

The Padstow Lifeboat: March for brass band Op.94 (1967)
Written to celebrate the launching of the new lifeboat near to the Trevose Head
lighthouse whose foghorn 'D' features throughout the piece
Duration 4'30"
First performance Black Dyke Mills Band/BMC Concert Band/Malcolm Arnold – Royal Festival
Hall, London, 10 June 1967 (BBC International Festival of Light Music, broadcast 'live' on
the Light Programme)
First Cornwall performance St Dennis Silver Band/Malcolm Arnold – Padstow Harbour, 19
July 1968*
Publisher Henrees Music, 1967; Studio Music

Catalogue of works

Notes *On the occasion of the planned visit of Princess Marina, President of the Royal
    National Lifeboat Institute to name the new lifeboat 'James and Catherine MacFarlane'.
    Unfortunately, Princess Marina was admitted to hospital only the day before the launch
    and, as a result, the Duke of Kent was invited in her place.
Article Professor Dr Charles E Scurrell, 'Sir Malcolm's Arnold's The Padstow Lifeboat Op.94
    – a study of the composer, the music and the lifeboats that inspired it' [in 4 parts] –
    Beckus 88, Spring 2013; *Beckus* 89, Summer 2013; *Beckus* 90, Autumn 2013; *Beckus* 91,
    Winter 2013

(a) arranged for military band by Ray Woodfield (1967)
Publisher Henrees Music, 1967

(b) arranged for eight brass instruments and percussion by Alan Civil (1984)
Instrumentation Tpt.(3), Hn.(2); Tbn.(2), Tba. Perc.
First performance Gabrieli Brass Ensemble – Royal Festival Hall, London, 19 December 1984
    (Christmas Concert)
Publisher Studio Music

(c) arranged for large orchestra by Philip Lane (2000)
Instrumentation 1+picc./2/2/1+cbsn. – 4/3/3/1 – timp.perc.(3) str
First performance City of Birmingham Symphony Orchestra/Rumon Gamba – Symphony Hall,
    Birmingham, 6 June 2001
First London performance Royal Philharmonic Orchestra/Robin Stapleton – Royal Albert Hall,
    London, 22 October 2005 (Battle of Trafalgar Proms)
First Europe performance Musikskolan Vanersborg, Sweden, 9 July 2008
First US performance Susquehanna Symphony Orchestra/Brian Folus – Bel Air High School,
    Maryland, 20 May 2017
Publisher Novello, 2000 (as Op.94a)
Notes This version of the March was played by the London Philharmonic Orchestra during
    the Thames Diamond Jubilee Pageant on 3 June 2012. It was timed to coincide with the
    arrival of the barge as it passed the Lifeboat Station on the Victoria Embankment close
    to Waterloo Bridge.

Symphony No.6 Op.95 (1967)
Duration 26'
Instrumentation 2+picc./2/2/2 – 4/3/3/1 – timp. perc.(3) hp. str.
First performance BBC Northern Symphony Orchestra/Malcolm Arnold – Sheffield City Hall,
    24 June 1968
First broadcast performance above performance – Radio 4, 28 June 1968
First London performance Royal Philharmonic Orchestra/Malcolm Arnold – Royal Albert Hall,
    London, 24 September 1969
First televised performance above performance – BBC Television, 4 April 1970
First Canada performance CBC Symphony Orchestra/Eric Wild – CBC Winnipeg, 8 June 1971
First Europe amateur performance Manchester Youth Orchestra – Église Saint-Médard de
    Thouars, Poitou-Charentes, France, 29 July 1984
First Europe professional performance Aarhus Conservatoire Orchestra/Douglas Bostock –
    Aarhus, Denmark, November 2001 (80th birthday celebration concert)
Publisher Faber, 1974

Notes The only symphony not to have been commissioned, the work also bears no dedication; however, the first movement pays homage to Charlie Parker, the great alto saxophonist of the Bebop era, and the slow movement has been described by the composer as "a lament for a pop style which will be dead before this symphony is performed".

Cowboy in Africa: theme music for the American TV series (1967)

Executive producers/writers: Andy White and Ivan Tors
Director: Andrew Marton
First broadcast performance 11 September 1967
Notes Arnold's theme is derived from the 'Swahili Serenade' he wrote as part of the soundtrack to the film 'Africa – Texas Style!' and was used for the first 16 (of 26) episodes.

Trevelyan: Suite for ten instruments Op.96 (1967)

[1. Palindrome 2. Nocturne 3. Apotheosis]
Written for the opening of Trevelyan College*, University of Durham, by Lord Butler
Duration 8'
Instrumentation 3Fl. 2Ob. 2Cl. 2Hn. Vc. (or 2 Bsn.)
First performance University of Durham Ensemble/Malcolm Arnold – Trevelyan College, University of Durham, 12 March 1968
First public performance Trianon Music Group/Chris Green – Ipswich Civic College, April 1971
First East Africa performance Nairobi Orchestra (wind section)/Jim Pywell – Ashwal Auditorium, Nairobi, Kenya, 24 May 2008
First US performance Treasure Coast Wind Ensemble – Vera Beach, Florida, 8 June 2018
Publisher Faber, 1970
Notes *Arnold's daughter Katherine was at that time an Undergraduate at the College.

(a) arranged for flute, oboe and piano by Paul Harris (2006)
First performance Intriplicate – Royal & Derngate, Northampton, 22 October 2006 (First Malcolm Arnold Festival)

Peterloo: Overture for orchestra Op.97 (1967)

Commissioned by the Trades Union Congress for the 100th anniversary of its first meeting in Manchester in June 1868.
Duration 9'45"
Instrumentation 2+picc./2/2/2 – 4/3/3/1 – timp. perc.(4) hp. str.
First performance Royal Philharmonic Orchestra/Malcolm Arnold – Royal Festival Hall, London, 7 June 1968
First televised performance above performance – BBC1, 9 June 1968
First performance (choral version with words by Tim Rice and vocal score arranged by Ben Parry), BBC Symphony Orchestra and Chorus/Sakari Oramo – Royal Albert Hall, London, 13 September 2014 (Promenade Concert)
Publisher Faber, 1979
Notes Peterloo refers to the infamous massacre which took place at St Peter's Fields, Manchester on 16 August 1819 – the new Bridgewater Hall is built on the site of the massacre; Arnold's overture was played there at a Royal Gala Concert by the Hallé

Orchestra conducted by Kent Nagano on 4 December 1996 celebrating both the composer's 75th birthday and the opening of the new hall.

(a) arranged for wind band by Charles Sayre (1979)
Publisher Studio Music/Hal Leonard

(b) arranged for wind band by Hisaatsu Kondo
First performance Kosei Wind Orchestra/Tochijuki Ise – Japan Band Festival, 1993

(c) arranged for wind band by Munetoshi Senoo
First performance Bunkyo University Wind Orchestra/Munetoshi Senoo

(d) arranged for brass band by Andrew Duncan (2002)
First performance Leyland Band/Michael Fowles – Bridgewater Hall, Manchester, 2002
First Australia performance Sellers International Band – ABC Classics FM, 4 March 2006
Publisher Faber
Notes There is also another (unpublished) brass band arrangement by Trevor Walmsley (c.2000), first performed by the Williams Fairey Band, conducted by James Gourlay – Symphony Hall, Birmingham, September 2000 (World of Brass Festival)

(e) Excerpt 'Theme' arranged for trumpet and piano by Deborah Callard
Publisher Trinity/Faber, in 'Trumpet All Sorts Grades 1-3'

This Christmas Night for unaccompanied SATB chorus (1967)
[Words: Mary Wilson*]
Written at the invitation of the *Daily Telegraph*
Duration 2'
First performance Kensington Consort – 10 Downing Street, London, 22 December 1967
First public performance Festival Singers/Bernard West – St Matthew's Church, Northampton, 18 October 2008 (Third Malcolm Arnold Festival)
Publisher Daily Telegraph Magazine, Issue No.168, 22 December 1967 'Mrs Wilson's Christmas Carol'; Faber, 1968; and re-produced in *Beckus* 23, Winter 1996
Notes *Wife of the then Prime Minister, Harold Wilson – the poem was included in a 1971 Pye LP recorded entitled 'Mrs Wilson reads her selected poems'.

The First Lady: opening and closing titles for BBC Television series (1968)
Duration 2'
Instrumentation 0/0/0/0 – 0/3/3/1 – perc.(2) cel. hp.(2) + SATB chorus
First broadcast performance – BBC Television, 7 April 1968 (the last episode was televised on 17 July 1969
Music played by: Studio Orchestra/Marcus Dods
Series Producer: David E Rose
Notes At the end of the series Arnold's theme was used in an arrangement for brass band by Ronnie Hazlehurst.

A Salute to Thomas Merritt for two brass bands and orchestra Op.98 (1967)
Written to celebrate the 60th anniversary of the death of the Cornish composer, Thomas Merritt
Duration 5'

Instrumentation 2+picc./2/2/2 – 4/3/3/1 – timp. perc.(4) hp. str.
First performance Penzance Orchestral Society/Cornwall Symphony Orchestra/St Dennis
    Silver Band/St Agnes Silver Band/Malcolm Arnold – Truro Cathedral, Cornwall, 16 March
    1968
First broadcast performance above performance – Radio 3, 17 April 1968
Articles (i) Ian Graham-Jones and Alan Poulton, 'Malcolm Arnold and Thomas Merritt' –
    Beckus 103, Winter 2016
(ii) Alan Poulton, 'Thomas Merritt' – *Maestro* 4, October 2017
(ii) Ian Graham-Jones, 'Salute to Thomas Merritt' (with music examples) – *Beckus* 109,
    Summer 2018

Hong Kong Anniversary Overture for orchestra Op.99 (1968)
Written for the 21st birthday of the Hong Kong Philharmonic Society
Duration 4'
Instrumentation 2/2/2/2 – 4/2/3/0 – timp. perc. str.
First performance Hong Kong Philharmonic Orchestra/Arrigo Foa – Hong Kong City Hall, 8
    December 1968
First broadcast performance BBC Northern Symphony Orchestra/Malcolm Arnold – Radio 3,
    18 December 1969 (recorded 28 October 1969)
First UK concert performance Orchestra of the Light Music Society/Malcolm Arnold – Royal
    Festival Hall, London, 17 December 1970 (South Bank 'Pops' Concert)
First US performance Charleston Symphony Orchestra – Charleston, South Carolina, 25
    September 1981
First Europe performance Stadtorchester Zug/Jonathan Brett-Hamilton – Zug, Switzerland,
    18 June 1999
First Japan performance Orchestra Sonore/Akira Endo – Nagano Civic Hall, 2 December 2007
Publisher Central Music Library, 1974; Faber, 1989 (as 'Anniversary Overture Op.99')

(a) arranged for wind band by Rodney Parker (2000)
First performance Royal Artillery Band/Major Stephen Smith (SRC recording)
Publisher Faber

Savile Centenary Fanfare for two trumpets (1968)
Written in celebration of the Savile Club centenary
Duration c.1'
First performance Trumpeters of the Brigade of Guards – Savile Club Ballroom, London, 30
    October 1968 (Savile Centenary Dinner)
First public performance Nick Bunker and Stephen Rapp (Tpts.) – Malcolm Arnold Academy,
    Northampton, 12 October 2019 (Fourteenth Malcolm Arnold Festival)
Publisher QTP
Notes The second half of the Fanfare is on one note for both players following the rhythmic
    pattern of the National Anthem!

St Endellion Ringers: Canon for voices (1968)
Written for the St Endellion Festival for performance in the church of St Endelienta (St
    Endellion), a few miles inland from Port Isaac in Cornwall.
Duration 30"
Notes Reproduced in *Maestro* 7, October 2020, p.55

Catalogue of works

Fantasy for trumpet Op.100 (1969)
Dedicated to Ernest Hall, Arnold's teacher at the Royal College of Music
Duration 4'
Publisher Faber, 1969
Article John Wallace, 'Fantasy for trumpet Op.100' (with music examples) – *Maestro* 3,
   October 2016

(a) arranged as Fantasy for trumpet and piano by Marlon Humphreys
Unpublished

Fantasy for trombone Op.101 (1969)
Duration 4'
Publisher Faber, 1969
Article Dan Jenkins, 'Fantasy for trombone, Op.101' (with music examples) – *Maestro* 3,
   October 2016

Fantasy for tuba Op.102 (1969)
Duration 4'
First performance John Fletcher, c.1969-70
First televised performance during a John Wallace Masterclass – BBC 2, 12 March 1990
Publisher Faber, 1969
Article John Elliott, 'Fantasy for tuba Op.102' (with music examples) – *Maestro* 3, October
   2016

The Song of Accounting Periods for high voice and piano Op.103 (1969)
[Words from the Finance Act 1965]
Commissioned by John Godber and John Gould for a touring recital programme 'The
Invisible Backwards Facing Grocer'
Duration 2'45"
First performance John Godber (Ten.)/John Gould (Pno.) – Manchester University, 17 April
   1969
First London performance above artists – Purcell Room, London, 4 May 1969
Publisher Novello, in 'Malcolm Arnold: Songs and Arias'
Notes The original title was 'The Song of Accountancy' and had a pianissimo ending!
Article Richard Shaw and John Gould 'The Song of Accounting Periods' – *Beckus* 51, Winter
   2003; *Maestro* 4, October 2017

Concerto for two pianos (3 hands) and orchestra Op.104 (1969)
Commissioned by the BBC and dedicated "To Phyllis and Cyril with affection and
admiration"
Duration 12'30"
Instrumentation 2+picc./2/2/2 – 4/3/3/1 – timp. perc.(2) hp. str.
Alt instrumentation 2/2/2/2 – 2/2/1/1 – timp. perc. hp. str.
First performance Phyllis Sellick/Cyril Smith/BBC Symphony Orchestra/Malcolm Arnold –
   Royal Albert Hall, London, 16 August 1969 (a Promenade Concert broadcast 'live' on
   Radio 2)*
First Australia performance Heidelberg Symphony Orchestra/Chris Kopke – Ivanhoe Girls'
   Grammar School, Melbourne, 24 June 2000

65

First Europe performance Jennifer Micaleff/Vladimir Ovchinikov/Britten Sinfonia/Nicholas Cleobury – Valletta, Malta, 1 July 2000

Publisher Faber, 1969

Notes (i) *The finale was encored – there is a recording of the premiere and encore at Stanford University, California in their Archive of Recorded Sound.

(ii) A recording of the second movement was used in a Michael Grandage production of Terence Rattigan's drama 'The Deep Blue Sea' at the Mercury Theatre, Colchester in April 1997. Coincidentally, the drama had also been made into a film in 1955, for which Arnold provided the musical soundtrack.

Article Daniel Adni, 'Malcolm Arnold's Concertos: masterpieces of mélange' (with music examples) – *Maestro* 5, October 2018

(a) arranged for two pianos (4 hands) and orchestra by Julian Elloway

Instrumentation 2/2/2/2 – 2/2/1/1 – timp. perc. hp. str.

First performance Richard Markham/David Nettle/BBC Concert Orchestra/Barry Wordsworth – Queen Elizabeth Hall, London, 26 October 1991 (60th birthday concert broadcast 'live' on Radio 2)

Publisher Faber, 1990

(b) arranged for piano duet (4 hands) and orchestra by Steven Worbey and Kevin Farrell (2011)

First performance Steven Worbey and Kevin Farrell/Young Musician's Symphony Orchestra/ James Blair – St John's Smith Square, London, November 2011

Article Steven Worbey and Kevin Farrell, 'Brighton Philharmonic Orchestra – Piano Concerto' – *Beckus* 108, Spring 2018

(c) also arranged for solo piano and orchestra by John Lenehan

(d) Excerpt 'Slow Movement Theme' arranged for clarinet and piano by Paul Harris

Publisher Faber, as 'Twilight' in 'Clarinet Basics'

[as a ballet] Hands: Ballet (1975) [using only the second movement of the concerto*]

Commissioned by the Royal Winnipeg Ballet Company

Choreographer: Paddy Stone

First performance Royal Winnipeg Ballet – National Arts Centre, Ottawa, Canada, 4 August 1975

Notes *The other six movements of the ballet are all concerned with different aspects of the human hand with music from Mozart, the Beatles and Eric Clapton.

Article Alan Poulton, 'Arnold's other ballets' – *Maestro* 4, October 2017

[as a ballet] 25: Ballet (2012) [using only the second and third movements]

Created in celebration of the 25th anniversary of the National Youth Ballet

Choreographer: Jo Meredith

First performance E M Forster Theatre, Tonbridge School, Tonbridge, Kent, 24-26 August 2012

First London performance Sadler's Wells Theatre, London, 2 September 2012 (Gala performance)

Articles (i) Anthony Meredith, 'A new Arnold ballet' – *Beckus* 85, Summer 2012

(ii) Alan Poulton, 'Arnold's other ballets' – *Maestro* 4, October 2017 [as a ballet] Concerto for Joyce and Dennis: Ballet (2017)

Choreographer: Matthew Hart (and dedicated to his grandparents, the subject of the ballet)

First performance Images Ballet Company, on a UK tour which took place between May and June 2017

Article Alan Poulton, 'Arnold's other ballets' – *Maestro 4*, October 2017

Songs for Julie Felix (1970s)

Notes In response to a letter from the composer in October 1993, Julie Felix replied, "I don't appear to have the songs that you wrote for me all those years ago." This somewhat enigmatic reply does not make it clear as to whether the songs went missing or whether they ever existed in the first place.

Concerto for 28 players Op.105 (1970)

Commissioned by the Stuyvesant Foundation and written specially for the English Chamber Orchestra.

Duration 22'

Instrumentation 1/2/0/1 – 2/0/0/0 – str. (6/6/4/4/2)

First performance English Chamber Orchestra/Malcolm Arnold – Queen Elizabeth Hall, London, 25 April 1970

First broadcast performance Northern Sinfonia/Steuart Bedford – Radio 3, 20 June 1979 (repeated 22 March 1980)

First Canada performance Manitoba Chamber Orchestra – Winnipeg, Manitoba, 18 December 1984

First US performance Miami University Chamber Orchestra – Miami University, Ohio, 30 January 1990

First Asia performance Macao Conservatory of Music Orchestra/En Shao – Beijing, China, 28 May 2005

First Europe performance Chamber Orchestra of Lapland – Ivalo Church, Finland, 11 February 2010

Publisher Faber, 1970

Articles (i) Piers Burton-Page, '28 and counting: a study in three movements' – *Beckus 96*, Spring 2015

(ii) Tony Meredith, 'Was the muse really missing?' – *Beckus 97*, Summer 2015

Fanfare for Louis for two trumpets (or two cornets) (1970)

Written for 'Louis Armstrong's 70th birthday with admiration and gratitude'

Duration 1'30"

First performance Elgar Howarth and Stanley Woods – Queen Elizabeth Hall, London, 4 July 1970 (Louis Armstrong 70th Birthday Concert sponsored by 'Melody Maker')

First broadcast performance The Wallace Collection – Radio 3, 14 March 1987 (a concert given on 30 August 1986 in the Queen's Hall as part of the Edinburgh International Festival)

Publisher Studio Music, 1986

Notes An augmented version of the Fanfare was played by the Silver Trumpets of the Royal Marines School of Music at the very first 'Filmharmonic' concert held at the Royal Albert Hall, London on 14 October 1970, in aid of the Cinema and Television Benevolent Fund

Malcolm Arnold

Fantasy for audience and orchestra Op.106 (1970)
Commissioned by the BBC for performance at the 'Last Night of the Proms'
Duration 13'30"
Instrumentation 2+picc./2/2/2 – 4/3/3/1 – timp. perc.(3) hp. organ str.
First performance BBC Symphony Orchestra/Colin Davis – Royal Albert Hall, London, 12
   September 1970 (a Promenade Concert broadcast 'live' on Radio 2)
Notes The work includes a traditional hornpipe in 5/4 time and includes the tune 'On the
   road to Freedom, we shall not be moved'
Article Christine Dyer, 'Fantasy for audience and orchestra' – Beckus 104, Spring 2017
Unpublished

Fantasy for guitar Op.107 (1970)
[Prelude – Scherzo – Arietta – Fughetta – Arietta – March – Postlude]
Written for and dedicated to Julian Bream
Duration 10'
First performance Julian Bream – Queen Elizabeth Hall, London, 16 May 1971
First televised performance Julian Bream – London Weekend Television, 12 June 1971 (in
   conversation with Humphrey Burton in the 'Aquarius' studios)
First broadcast performance Julian Bream – Radio 3, 5 May 1975
Publisher Faber, 1971 (ed. Julian Bream)
Articles (i) Sean Shibe, 'Fantasy for guitar' – Beckus 107, Winter 2017
(ii) Piers Burton-Page, in 'Malcolm Arnold and Julian Bream' – Maestro 7, October 2020

Concerto for viola and chamber orchestra Op.108 (1971)
Commissioned by Northern Arts and dedicated to the Northern Sinfonia and Roger Best
(their principal viola)
Duration 20'
Instrumentation 1/2/2/2 – 2/0/0/0 – str.
First performance Roger Best/Northern Sinfonia/Malcolm Arnold – Carlisle Market Hall, 13
   October 1971 (Newcastle Festival)
First London performance above artists – Queen Elizabeth Hall, London, 15 October 1971
First broadcast performance above artists – Radio 3, 3 May 1972 (rec. 18 October 1971)
First Canada performance John Barnum/Oakville Chamber Orchestra – Central Baptist
   Church, Oakville, Ontario, 27 May 2001
First Europe performance Michele Santorsola/Orchestra Sinfonica Siciliana – Palermo, Sicily,
   11 July 2001
First Australia performance Asyln Keck/Toowomba Concert Orchestra/Martin Cook –
   University of South Queensland, Toowomba, Queensland, 17 October 2004
Publisher Faber, 1992 (also arranged for viola and piano, 1980)
Notes (i) As early as 1959 Arnold had intimated to Roy Plomley on 'Desert Island Discs' that
   he was writing a viola concerto for William Primrose.
(ii) BBC 2's 'Music Now' series (introduced by John Amis) filmed Arnold directing
   performances of his Viola Concerto both in Carlisle and Newcastle-upon-Tyne. The
   programme was televised on 9 January 1972.
Articles (i) Günther Kögebehn and Simon Ballard 'St Paul's Sinfonia: Viola Concerto' – Becku
   105, Summer 2017
(ii) Rooke, Paul Adrian 'Two rarely heard Concertos' – Beckus 111, Winter 2018

Catalogue of works

Fanfare for one, eighty years young: for solo trumpet (1971)
Duration 10"
Commissioned by the Council and Chairman of the Composer's Guild in celebration of the eightieth birthday of their President, Sir Arthur Bliss and to whom the Fanfare is dedicated "with admiration, respect and affection".
Among the other British composers who provided musical birthday greetings were William Alwyn, Lennox Berkeley, Benjamin Britten, Alan Bush, Geoffrey Bush, Arnold Cooke, Elizabeth Maconchy, Edmund Rubbra, Humphrey Searle and Grace Williams.

Popular Birthday for orchestra: composite work (1972)
Commissioned by André Previn and the London Symphony Orchestra and written "for the seventieth birthday of Sir William Walton* OM, with homage and every expression of friendship" – the other composers were Richard Rodney Bennett, Thea Musgrave, Robert Simpson, Nicholas Maw and Peter Maxwell Davies.
Duration 1'
Instrumentation 1+2 picc./2/2/2 – 4/3/3/1 – timp. perc.(2) hp. str.
First performance London Symphony Orchestra/Malcolm Arnold – Royal Festival Hall, London, 28 March 1972 (Walton's 70th Birthday Concert)

also arranged for chamber ensemble
Instrumentation Fl. Pno. Perc.(2) Vn. Vn. Va. Vc.
First performance Nash Ensemble/Marcus Dods – BBC 2 Television, 29 March 1972 ('Walton at 70')
Notes *The work contains a quotation from Walton's 'Popular Song' from Façade

Song of Freedom for SA chorus and brass band Op.109 (1972)
[1. Prelude (Maureen Parr, Nina Truzka, Susan Selwyn)
2. Hymn (Vivienne McClean)
3. Intermezzo (Diana Henry, Caroline Richardson)
4. Postlude (John Michael Thompson, Maureen Parr)]
Duration 19'
Commissioned by and dedicated to the National School Brass Band Association (NSBBA) in celebration of their 21st anniversary.
First performance Netteswell School Band and Choir/Malcolm Arnold – Harlow Sports Centre, 12 May 1973
First broadcast performance above performance – Radio 3, 5 November 1973
First London performance Harrow Schools' Girls' Choir/GUS (Footwear) Band/Geoffrey Brand – Royal Albert Hall, London, 6 October 1973 (National Brass Band Championships of Great Britain Festival Concert)
Publisher Henrees Music, 1972; Studio Music (vocal score)
Notes The words were chosen by the composer from poems on freedom written by children as part of a nationwide competition sponsored by the NSBBA.

The Fair Field Overture for orchestra Op.110 (1972)
Commissioned by Croydon Arts Festival for the tenth anniversary of the opening of the Fairfield Hall* and dedicated to "William Walton with the greatest esteem and affection".
Duration 7'30"
Instrumentation 2+picc./3/3/3 – 4/3/3/1 – timp. perc.(2) str.

First performance Royal Philharmonic Orchestra/Malcolm Arnold – Fairfield Hall, Croydon, Surrey, 27 April 1973

First broadcast performance BBC Symphony Orchestra/Malcolm Arnold – Radio 3, 16 March 1977 (recorded Studio 1, Maida Vale, 10 April 1976)

Publisher Faber/Central Music Library, 1973

Notes *The Fairfield Halls were built on the site of the old Fair Field in Croydon – the composer writes, "in [this] overture … I have attempted to create the atmosphere of a pastoral fair field, with overtones of a funfair field, by means of one long theme heard in various guises [following] the historical events that have taken place [there]."

(a) arranged for wind band by Rodney Parker (2002)
Publisher Faber

[as a ballet] (2002)
Choreographer: Petal Miller Ashmole
First performance Singapore Dance Theatre – Esplanade Theatres on the Bay, University of Singapore, 12-15 December 2002

Concerto No.2 for flute and chamber orchestra Op.111 (1972)
Written for and dedicated to Richard Adeney
Duration 14'
Instrumentation 0/2/0/0 – 2/0/0/0 – str.
First performance Richard Adeney/English Chamber Orchestra/Kenneth Sillito – The Maltings, Snape, 28 June 1973 (Aldeburgh Festival)
First London performance Richard Adeney/English Chamber Orchestra/Wilfried Boettcher – Queen Elizabeth Hall, London, 1 October 1973
First broadcast performance Peter Lloyd/London Symphony Orchestra/André Previn – Radio 3, 9 August 1974 (a Promenade Concert broadcast 'live' from the Royal Albert Hall, London)
First Canada performance Winnipeg Symphony Orchestra – Winnipeg, Manitoba, 26 January 1985
First US performance California State University – Long Beach, California, 18 February 2000
Publisher Faber, 1973 (also arranged for flute and piano, 1978)

A Flourish for orchestra Op.112 (1973)
Written to celebrate the 500th anniversary of the Charter of the City of Bristol
Duration 3'30"
Instrumentation 2+picc./2/2/2 – 4/3/3/1 – timp. perc.(3) str.
First performance Bournemouth Symphony Orchestra/Rudolf Schwarz – Colston Hall, Bristol, 26 September 1973
First US performance New Philharmonic Orchestra of Irving – Irving, Texas, 20 October 1990
First London performance BBC Concert Orchestra/Barry Wordsworth – Queen Elizabeth Hall, London, 26 October 1991 (70th Birthday Concert broadcast 'live' on Radio 2)
First Europe performance Aalborg Symphony Orchestra/Owain Arwel Hughes – Aalborg, Denmark, 4 January 1997
Publisher Faber, 1973

Catalogue of works

(a) arranged for symphonic wind band by Guy Wolfenden (2001) at the request of Faber Music

First performance Birmingham Conservatoire Wind Orchestra/Guy Wolfenden – Levi Fox Hall, Stratford-upon-Avon, 16 October 2001 (Sixth English Music Festival Concert celebrating the composer's 80th birthday)

Publisher Faber, 2001

Symphony No.7 Op.113 (1973)

[1. Katherine 2. Robert 3. Edward]

Commissioned by the New Philharmonia Trust and dedicated to Arnold's children (each of the three movements is a musical portrait).

Duration 45'

Instrumentation 2+picc.2/2/2+cbsn. – 4/3/3/1 – timp. perc.(3) hp. str.

First performance New Philharmonia Orchestra/Malcolm Arnold – Royal Festival Hall, London, 5 May 1974

First broadcast performance BBC Symphony Orchestra/Malcolm Arnold – Radio 3, 16 March 1977

Publisher Faber, 1974, 1991

First US performance Orange County High School of the Arts Orchestra/Chris Russell – Margaret A Webb Theatre, Orange County, California, 24 May 1999

First Europe performance Aarhus Conservatoire Orchestra/Douglas Bostock – Aarhus, Denmark, November 2001 (80th birthday Concert)

Articles (i) John Pearce, 'The Seventh – Live!' – *Beckus* 59, Winter 2005

(ii) Howard Sowerby, 'The Cowbell Symphony' – *Beckus* 61, Summer 2006

(iii) Michael Jameson, 'New recording of the Seventh Symphony' – *Beckus* 95, Spring 2015

Fantasy for brass band Op.114a (1973)

[Prelude – Dance – Elegy – Scherzo – Postlude]

Written as the test piece for the 1974 National Brass Band Championships and dedicated to Tony Giles.

Duration 10'

First performance Cory Band/Major H A Kenney – Royal Albert Hall, London, 5 October 1974 (National Brass Band Championships)

First broadcast performance above performance – Radio 3, 21 October 1974 (the composer's 53rd birthday)

Publisher Henrees Music, 1974; Studio Music

Two John Donne Songs for tenor and piano Op.114b (1974)

[1. The Good-Morrow 2. Woman's Constancy]

Duration 6'

Dedication: 'for Niamh'

First performance Ian Partridge (Ten.)/Jennifer Partridge (Pno.) – Bristol University, 23 June 1977

First broadcast performance above performance – Radio 3, 20 October 1977

First London performance above artists – Purcell Room, London, 28 March 1996

Publisher Roberton, 1977; Novello, in 'Malcolm Arnold: Songs and Arias'

Notes There is a sketch for a third song 'The Dreame' which was premiered at the Twelfth Malcolm Arnold Festival at the Royal & Derngate, Northampton, on 15 October 2017 by Claire Thompson (Sop.) and Scott Mitchell (Pno.)

Concerto No.2 for clarinet and chamber orchestra Op.115 (1974)

Written for and dedicated to Benny Goodman 'with admiration and affection' – the third movement is subtitled 'Pre-Goodman Rag'.

Duration 17'30"

Instrumentation 1+picc./2/0/2 – 2/0/0/0 – timp. perc. str.

First performance Benny Goodman/Denver Symphony Orchestra/Brian Priestman – Red Rocks, Denver, Colorado, USA, 17 August 1974 (Red Rocks Music Festival)

First UK performance Benny Goodman/Park Lane Music Players/Malcolm Arnold – St John's Smith Square, London, 11 October 1976 (at a gala concert to support St John's and the Park Lane Group, and given in the presence of Princess Margaret)

First Japan performance Kokubunji Philharmonic Orchestra/Seiji Sagawa – Tokyo, 24 November 1996

First Australia performance Nick McRoberts/Victoria Youth Symphony Orchestra/Toby Bell – St Mary's Church, Melbourne, 23 October 1999

First Russia performance Michael Collins/Russian National Orchestra/Mikhail Pletnev – Moscow, 13 September 2009

First New Zealand performance Kiara Kong/Auckland Youth Orchestra – Auckland Town Hall, 18 October 2020

Publisher Faber, 1984 (full score) (also arranged for clarinet and piano, 1981)

Notes There is a specially composed cadenza for the first movement by Richard Rodney Bennett – the cadenza was first heard at the 'Last Night of the Proms' on 11 September 1993, played by Michael Collins who had commissioned it. The concert was televised by the BBC.

Articles (i) Daniel Adni, 'Malcolm Arnold's Concertos: masterpieces of mélange' (with musical examples) – *Maestro* 5, October 2018

(ii) Eleanor Fox, 'Just Great: Malcolm Arnold's Clarinet Concerto No.2 Op.115' (with music examples) – *Maestro* 5, October 2018

(a) Excerpt 'The Pre-Goodman Rag' arranged for clarinet and wind band by Guy Wolfenden (2000)

Duration 3'

First performance Linda Merrick (Cl.)/Birmingham Symphonic Winds/Keith Allen – CBSO Centre, Birmingham, 23 June 2001

First Europe performance Birmingham Symphonic Winds/Guy Wolfenden – Lucerne, Switzerland, 12 July 2001 (during WASBWE Festival)

First Asia performance Philharmonic Winds/Leonard Tan – Esplanade Theatres on the Bay, University of Singapore, 20 December 2017

Publisher Faber, 2000

[as a ballet] (2006)

Choreographer: Odessa Munroe

First performance Brno Philharmonic Orchestra – Brno, Czech Republic, 23-24 March 2006

Piano Sonata [No.2] (1975)

Notes In a letter dated 21 March 1975 to David Drew, Malcolm intimated that he was "working on a piano sonata" ['Rogue Genius' p.69]. The score is lost.

Fantasy on a theme of John Field for piano and orchestra Op.116 (1975)

Dedicated to John Lill
Duration 20'
Instrumentation 2+picc./2/2/2 – 4/3/3/1 – timp. perc.(2) hp. str.
First performance John Lill/Royal Philharmonic Orchestra/Lawrence Foster – Royal Festival Hall, London, 26 May 1977
First broadcast performance Martin Roscoe/BBC Philharmonic Orchestra/Edward Downes – Radio 3, 21 October 1986 (65th Birthday Concert)
First Europe performance Phillip Dyson/National Symphony Orchestra of Ireland/Howard Shelley – National Concert Hall, Dublin, 28 September 2001 (Malcolm Arnold's 80th Birthday Concert)
First Asia performance Djong Victorin Yu/Daegu Symphony Orchestra/Soo Hyun Yoo – Daegu Cultural Centre, Daegu, South Korea, 4 October 2002
Publisher Faber, 1975, 1994
Notes The theme is the 'Nocturne in C major' for solo piano – one of his mother's favourite pieces.
Articles (i) Paul Serotsky, 'Perspectives' – *Beckus* 33, Summer 1999
(ii) Paul Jackson, 'Fantasy on a theme of John Field', an extract from his book 'The Brilliant and the Dark' – *Beckus* 47, Winter 2002
(iii) Phillip Dyson, in 'Malcolm's piano music' – *Beckus* 108, Spring 2018

Railway Fanfare for 6 trumpets (1975)

Commissioned by the British Railways Board in celebration of the 150th anniversary of railways in Britain.
Duration 1'30"
First performance at the London Parks Exhibition of Stevenson's 'Rocket' in 1975
First broadcast performance The Wallace Collection – Radio 3, 14 March 1987 (a concert given on 30 August 1986 in the Queen's Hall as part of the Edinburgh International Festival)
Publisher Studio Music, 1986 (as No.3 of 'Four Fanfares')

Fantasy for harp Op.117 (1975)

Dedicated to Osian Ellis
Duration 11'
First performance Osian Ellis – Law Society Hall, London, 27 January 1976
First broadcast performance Osian Ellis – Radio 3, 8 May 1978 (recorded Studio 1, Birmingham, 11 October 1977)
Publisher Faber, 1978 (edited by Osian Ellis)
Articles (i) Keziah Thomas, 'Fantasy for harp Op.117' (with music examples) – *Maestro* 4, October 2017
(ii) Osian Ellis, 'Fantasy for harp' (with music examples) – *Maestro* 5, October 2018

The Three Musketeers: Ballet [sketches] (1975)

In 1975 the long-serving Royal Ballet dancer David Drew, branching out into choreography, started writing (as a private venture) a scenario for a full-length ballet of *The Three Musketeers*, in which he soon interested the stage designer Terence Emery. The pair enjoyed a relaxed meeting in a luxury London hotel with Arnold, from which some musical sketches survive. Unfortunately, when the secret project came to the ears of Kenneth MacMillan (the choreographer who at that time was also the Royal Ballet's Artistic Director), it was rejected out of hand. Although Robert Helpmann, the Artistic Director of the Australian Ballet, subsequently expressed some interest, there were problems with the ever-changing scenario, Arnold withdrew, and the project died an immediate death. Some good, if fairly sketchy, musical ideas had been presented at the hotel meeting, attempting to express the characters of the novel's main figures, and Arnold is said to have extemporised brilliantly as the champagne flowed, but that was the one and only occasion that Arnold, Drew and Emery ever met. Arnold never started tackling Drew's scenario, which was full of intricate detail and, at the time, far from complete. At that very difficult period in his life, Arnold would have struggled with the challenge of Drew's ambitious concept, had he not, very sensibly, opted out.

The (piano) sketches are as follows:

[1. Academy Theme ('One for all, all for one'), 2. D'Artagnan, 3. D'Artagnan combined with
the Academy Theme, 4. Aramis, 5. La Folia – Dance of Intrigue, 6. Porthos, 7. Athos,
8. The King, 9. M. Bonacieux, 10. The Cardinal, 11. Milady, 12. Buckingham, 13.
Constance's Sad Dance*, 14. Rochefort, 15. Musketeer's Dance.
N.B. the last two movements are fragmentary]

First public performance (sketches, omitting Nos.3 and 5) Moritz Ernst (Pno.) – Royal &
Derngate, Northampton, 16 October 2010 (Fifth Malcolm Arnold Festival)
Notes *Used as part of the slow movement of the Flute Sonata Op.121 and later
orchestrated to become part of the composite ballet 'The Three Musketeers' in 2006.
(see Appendix A)
Articles (i) Günther Kögebehn, a review of Raphael Thöne's thesis 'Malcolm Arnold – a
composer of real music' – *Beckus* 67, Winter 2007; *Maestro* 6, October 2019
(ii) Raphael Thöne, 'Elgar's influence on Malcolm Arnold' (with music examples) – *Maestro*
5, October 2018

String Quartet No.2 Op.118 (1975)

Dedicated to Hugh Maguire* who was then the first violin in the Allegri String Quartet
Duration 29'
First performance Allegri String Quartet – Hugh Maguire (Vn.), David Roth (Vn.), Patrick
Ireland (Va.), Bruno Schrecker (Vc.) – Dublin Castle, 9 June 1976
First UK performance Allegri String Quartet – The Maltings, Snape, 12 June 1976 (Aldeburgh
Festival)
First broadcast performance above (Aldeburgh) performance – Radio 3, 25 January 1980
First US performance Miami University Quartet – Oxford, Ohio, 29 January 1990
First London performance McCapra String Quartet – Ranger's House, Greenwich, 19
September 1992
First Europe performance Zsuzsa Debre Quartet – Moyland Castle, Germany, 15 January 2006
First Russia performance Nevsky Quartet – St Petersburg, October 2007 (British Music
Festival)

Publisher Faber, 1976

Notes *Maguire, a native of Ireland and, like Arnold, a Dublin resident, is given the opportunity to display his skills as a cèilidh fiddler in the quartet's second movement.

Articles (i) David Angel, '3h Malcolm Arnold's String Quartets' – *Beckus* 54, Autumn 2004; *Maestro* 5, October 2018

(ii) Piers Burton-Page, 'The Arnold Quartets revisited' (with music examples) – *Maestro* 5, October 2018

(a) arranged for solo violin and string orchestra by David Matthews (2005)

First performance Manning Camerata/Peter Manning – Waltham Abbey Church, Essex, 16 April 2005

First London performance Orchestra of St Paul's/Ben Palmer – St Paul's Church, Covent Garden, 23 March 2014

Publisher Faber, as 'Sonata for strings Op.118a (2005)'

Article Michael Jameson, 'Sonata for strings first recording' – *Beckus* 97, Summer 2015

The Return of Odysseus: Cantata for SATB chorus and orchestra Op.119 (1976)

[Words: Patric Dickinson]
Commissioned by the Schools' Music Association
Duration 30'
Instrumentation 2/2/2/2 – 4/3/3/1 – timp. perc.(2) hp. str.
First performance Schools' Music Association Choirs/Royal College of Music Symphony Orchestra/Sir David Willcocks – Royal Albert Hall, London, 24 April 1977
First US performance Mississippi Valley Chamber Orchestra and Chorus – St Paul, Minnesota, 1 June 1986
First Europe performance Stanislas College Orchestra and Chorus/Ad van Unen – Delft, Netherlands, 22 April 1995
Publisher Faber, 1976 (vocal score)
Article Paul Serotsky, 'The Return of Odysseus' – *Beckus* 61, Summer 2006; *Maestro* 6, October 2019

Philharmonic Concerto for orchestra Op.120 (1976)

[1. Intrada 2. Aria 3. Chacony]
Commissioned by the Commercial Union Assurance Company for the London Philharmonic Orchestra's bi-centennial tour of the USA in 1976 sponsored by Columbia Artists Management
Duration 15'
Instrumentation 2+picc./2+ca./2/2+cbsn. – 4/3/3/1 – timp. perc.(3) hp. str.
First performance London Philharmonic Orchestra/Bernard Haitink – Royal Festival Hall, London, 31 October 1976 (broadcast 'live' on Radio 3)
First US performance above artists – Chicago, 7 November 1976*
First Europe performance BBC Philharmonic Orchestra/Edward Downes – May 1987 (during a tour of Tulle, Clermont-Ferrand and Nimes)
Publisher Faber, 1976
Notes *The first New York performance took place in Carnegie Hall on 22 November 1976.

Sonata for flute and piano Op.121 (1977)

[I. Allegro II. Andantino III. Maestro con molto]
Commissioned by the Welsh Arts Council and dedicated to James Galway
Duration 14'
First performance James Galway (Fl.)/Anthony Goldstone (Pno.) – New Hall, Cardiff, 19
    March 1977 (Cardiff Festival)
First broadcast performance Richard Adeney (Fl.)/David Johns (Pno.) – Radio 3, 19 October
    1981
First London performance Helen Cawthorne (Fl.)/Lianne Barnard (Pno.) – British Music
    Information Centre, London, 27 September 1994
First Europe performance Gabriella Sinay (Fl.)/Raphael Thöne (Pno.) – Moyland Castle,
    Germany, 15 January 2006
Publisher Faber, 1980

Hard Times: ITV theme music (1977)

[Charles Dickens, adapted for television by Arthur Hopcraft]
Instrumentation 3 Fl. Ca. 2 Hn. 3 Tpt. 3 Tbn. Timp. Perc.
Music played by: Ensemble/Marcus Dods
First broadcast performance Granada Television, 25 October 1977 (later transmitted on
    WNET Channel 13 in New York)
    Producer: Peter Eckersley
    Director: John Irvin
Notes This is an arrangement by Marcus Dods of the 'Cavatina' from the Little Suite for
    brass band Op.93 q.v.

Variations for orchestra on a theme of Ruth Gipps Op.122 (1977)

Duration 13'
Instrumentation 1+picc./2/2/2 – 2/2/0/0/ – timp. str.
First performance Chanticleer Orchestra/Ruth Gipps – Queen Elizabeth Hall, London, 22
    February 1978
First US performance Miami University Chamber Orchestra – Miami University, Oxford, Ohio,
    30 January 1990
Publisher Faber, 1978, 2001
Notes The theme is from Ruth Gipps's Coronation March of 1953
Article Alan Poulton, 'Malcolm Arnold and Ruth Gipps' – *Beckus* 100, Spring 2016

Symphony for brass instruments Op.123 (1978)

Written for the Philip Jones Brass Ensemble and dedicated to Philip Jones on his fiftieth
birthday
Duration 30'
Instrumentation 4 Tpt. 4Hn. 4 Tbn. Tba.
First performance Philip Jones Brass Ensemble/Howard Snell – Cheltenham Town Hall, 8 July
    1979 (Cheltenham Festival)
First broadcast performance above performance – Radio 3, 20 October 1979
First London performance Philip Jones Brass Ensemble/Howard Snell – Queen Elizabeth Hall,
    London, 16 March 1980
First US performance Wisconsin Brass Ensemble – Madison, Wisconsin, 9 October 1983

Catalogue of works

First Europe broadcast performance Radio Sweden, 4 November 1986
First Europe concert performance London Brass Virtuosi – San Sebastian-Donostia, Spain, 7
    September 1991
First Canada performance Brass Roots – London, Ontario, 31 March 1991
Publisher Faber, 1978, 1983

Symphony No.8 Op.124 (1978)
Commissioned by the Rustan K Kermani Foundation in memory of Rustan K Kermani*
Duration 25'
Instrumentation 2+picc./2/2/2 – 4/3/3/1 – timp. perc.(2) hp. str.
First performance Albany Symphony Orchestra/Julius Hegyi – Troy Savings Bank Music Hall,
    Albany, New York, USA, 5 May 1979
First UK performance BBC Northern Symphony Orchestra/Sir Charles Groves – Royal
    Northern College of Music, Manchester, 2 October 1981
First broadcast performance above (Manchester) performance – Radio 3, 4 June 1982
First London performance Young Musicians' Symphony Orchestra/James Blair – St John's
    Smith Square, London, 26 November 1982
First New Zealand performance Hampshire County Youth Orchestra/Edgar Holmes –
    Auckland Town Hall, 2 August 1993 (and broadcast on Radio 3, 18 February 1994)
First Europe performance Liszt Music Academy Orchestra – University of Miskoic, Hungary,
    27 October 1993
Publisher Faber, 1981
Notes (i) *Edmund Rubbra's Sinfonietta for strings and George Lloyd's Eleventh and Twelfth
    Symphonies have also been commissioned by this American Foundation
(ii) Richard Hickox was slated to conduct the first London professional performance of
    Symphony No.8 (at the Barbican Hall with the London Symphony Orchestra on 8 March
    1994) but it was replaced at the last minute by Symphony No.2.

(a) arranged for wind band by Munetoshi Senoo
First performance Bunkyo University Wind Orchestra/Munetoshi Senoo – Tokyo

Concerto for trumpet and orchestra Op.125 (1982)
Commissioned by the Arts Council of Great Britain in celebration of the 100th anniversary of
the founding of the Royal College of Music in 1883 and written for John Wilbraham
Duration 8'
Instrumentation 2/2/2/2 – 4/2/3/1 – timp. perc.(2) hp. str.
First performance John Wallace/Royal College of Music Great Gala Orchestra/Sir Alexander
    Gibson – Royal Albert Hall, London, 30 January 1983
First televised performance Ian Balmain/Royal College of Music Symphony Orchestra/Russell
    Keable – BBC Television, 23 May 1983 (a Gala Concert given in the presence of the Prince
    and Princess of Wales and broadcast 'live' from the Royal Albert Hall, London)
First US performance John Wallace/Tucson Symphony Orchestra – Tucson, Arizona, 3 August
    1991
First Ireland performance John Wallace/National Symphony Orchestra of Ireland/Brian
    Wright – National Concert Hall, Dublin, 6 February 1992
Publisher Faber, 1982 (full score); (also arranged for trumpet and piano, 1983)
Article John Wallace, 'Trumpet Concerto' (with music examples) – *Maestro* 3, October 2016

77

(a) arranged for trumpet and brass band by Tony Rickard (1998)
First performance soloist/Black Dyke Mills Band – Dukes Hall, Royal Academy of Music, London, 29 October 1998
Unpublished

Four Irish Dances for orchestra Op.126 (1982 and 1986)

Dedicated to Donald Mitchell, the then Chairman of Faber Music
Duration 11'
Instrumentation 2+picc./2/2/2 – 4/3/3/1 – timp. perc.(2) hp. str.
First performance London Philharmonic Orchestra/Malcolm Arnold – Lyrita recording studios, 27-28 October 1986)
First public performance Wren Orchestra/Malcolm Arnold – Leeds Castle, Kent, 10 October 1987 (Leeds Castle Festival)
First London performance Wren Orchestra/Iain Sutherland – Kenwood House, London, 18 June 1988 (English Heritage Lakeside Concert)
First broadcast performance Ulster Orchestra/Simon Jolly – Radio 3, 19 May 1990 (recorded 2 March 1989)
First US performance Rochester Philharmonic Orchestra/Peter Bay – Eastman Theatre, Eastman School of Music, University of Rochester, New York, 31 March 1995
First Asia performance RTE National Symphony Orchestra – Hong Kong, 10 August 1996
First New Zealand performance Auckland Philharmonic Orchestra/Samuel Wong – Aotea Centre, Auckland, 23 October 1997
First Canada performance Kamloops Symphony Orchestra – Kamloops, British Columbia, 8 November 1997
First Europe performance un-named orchestra and conductor – Mädchengymnasium St Agnes, Stuttgart, Germany, 1 June 1998
First Japan performance Kansai Philharmonic Orchestra – Izumi Hall, Osaka, 7 March 2004
Publisher Faber, 1986

(a) arranged for recorder ensemble by Denis Bloodworth (2003)
Unpublished

(b) arranged for wind quintet by Jonathan Whiting (2016)
First performance Lowry Quintet – Royal & Derngate, Northampton, 15 October 2016 (Eleventh Malcolm Arnold Festival)

(c) Dance No.3 arranged for flute and piano by Sally Adams
Publisher Faber, in 'Flute Basics'

[as a ballet] Alice in Wonderland: Ballet (1993)
Choreography: Toni Pimble
First performance Eugene Ballet Company – Eugene, Oregon, USA, 20 February 1993 (later revived by the Washington Ballet Company, Washington DC, USA, on 5 February 1996)
Notes The ballet also includes music by Grainger, Britten and Walton.

Fantasy for descant recorder Op.127 (1986)

Commissioned by Wingfield Arts and Music, and dedicated to Michala Petri
Duration 11'
First performance Michala Petri – St Michael's Church, Beccles, 11 July 1987

Catalogue of works

First US performance Michala Petri – State University of New York at Buffalo – Buffalo, New York, 1 March 1989 (with a performance at the Metropolitan Museum of Art in New York City later in the month)
First London performance Catherine Sing – Amaryllis Fleming Concert Hall, Royal College of Music, London, 13 May 1992
Publisher Faber, 1986
Article Michala Petri, 'Working with Malcolm Arnold' – *Maestro* 7, October 2020

Symphony No.9 Op.128 (1986)

Written for the BBC Philharmonic Orchestra and dedicated to Anthony John Day
Duration 52'30"
Instrumentation 2+picc./2/2/2 – 4/3/3/1 – timp. perc.(2) hp. str.
First performance (last movement Excerpt only) BBC Concert Orchestra/Malcolm Arnold – BBC Television, October 1991 (an 'Omnibus' documentary, recorded between 1-5 July 1991, celebrating the composer's seventieth birthday and directed by Kriss Rusmanis)*
First performance (complete) BBC Philharmonic Orchestra/Sir Charles Groves – Studio 7, BBC Manchester, 20 January 1992 (invitation concert for the Friends of the BBC Philharmonic Orchestra)**
First broadcast performance above BBC Manchester performance – Radio 3, 19 April 1992 (and repeated 23 March 1993)
First London performance London Festival Orchestra/Ross Pople – Royal Festival Hall, London, 19 October 1996 (75th Birthday Concert)
First US performance Susquehanna Symphony Orchestra/Sheldon Bair – John Carroll School, Bel Air, Maryland, 11 March 2000
Publisher Novello, 1990
Notes (i) *This BBC Music and Arts Production 'Malcolm Arnold at 70' was presented by the director at the Royal Academy of Music, London, on 18 June 1996 as part of the British and American Film Music Festival.
(ii) **The symphony's premiere (Bournemouth Symphony Orchestra/Sir Charles Groves) was originally planned to take place between 16-20 October 1991, with the first performance at Poole, followed by Bristol, Southampton and the Norfolk & Norwich Festival.
Articles (i) Piers Burton-Page, 'Symphony No.9' – *Beckus* 3, April 1992; *Maestro* 1, October 2014
(ii) Piers Burton-Page, 'The dilemma of the Ninth' – *Beckus* 83, Winter 2011
(iii) David Dunstan: 'Ealing Symphony Orchestra: The Ninth Symphony' – *Beckus* 99, Winter 2015

Three Fantasies for piano Op.129 (1986)

Dedicated to Eileen Gilroy (Thomas)
Duration 4'15"
First performance Kate Setchell – Assembly House, Norwich, 18 April 1987 (Easter Concert in aid of Norwich Cancer Relief Society)
Publisher QTP

[as a ballet] **Three Fantasies: Ballet (1995)**
Choreographer: Paul Jackson

First performance Paul Jackson (Pno.) – Ham Hall, University of Nevada, Las Vegas, Nevada, USA, 19 April 1995

Fantasy for cello Op.130 (1987)

Commissioned by and dedicated to Julian Lloyd Webber
Duration 16'
First performance Julian Lloyd Webber – Wigmore Hall, London, 13 December 1987
First broadcast performance Julian Lloyd Webber – Radio 3, 22 November 1989
First Europe performance Gudrun Schröder – Galerie Löhrl, Mönchengladbach, Germany, 4 June 2005
Publisher Faber, 1988
Article Julian Lloyd Webber, 'Fantasy for cello' – *Beckus* 109, Summer 2018

Little Suite No.3 for brass band Op.131 (1987)

Commissioned by Keith Wilson and dedicated to the Brass Band of Salford College of Technology (later University College Salford)
Duration 10'
First performance Salford College of Technology Brass Band/Roy Newsome – Maxwell Hall, Salford College of Technology, 4 November 1987 (L S Lowry Centenary Festival Concert)
First London performance Desford Colliery Dowty Band/Geoffrey Brand – Queen Elizabeth Hall, London, 12 November 1989
Publisher Studio Music, 1988
Article Paul Jackson, 'Little Suite No.3' (with music examples) – *Beckus* 7, January 1993; *Maestro* 1, October 2014

Brass Quintet No.2 Op.132 (1987)

Commissioned by the Fine Arts Brass Ensemble with funds provided by the British Reserve Insurance Co Ltd.
Duration 8'
Instrumentation 2 Tpt. Hn. Tbn. Tba.
First performance Fine Arts Brass Ensemble – Pittville Pump Room, Cheltenham, 11 July 1988 (Cheltenham Festival concert broadcast 'live' on Radio 3)
First Europe performance above artists – Bremen Radio, Germany, 9 October 1988
First London performance above artists – Wigmore Hall, London, 23 January 1989
First televised performance above artists – Central Television, 7 February 1989*
First New Zealand performance New Zealand Brass Quintet – Wellington, 9 March 1990
Notes *A documentary entitled 'An Act of Friendship' in the 'Contrasts' series directed by Terry Bryan – it featured performances of both Brass Quintets and an interview with the composer conducted by Piers Burton-Page.
Publisher Faber, 1988

Concerto for recorder and chamber orchestra Op.133 (1988)

Commissioned by the English Sinfonia with funds provided by Eastern Arts Association and dedicated to Michala Petri.
Duration 14'
Instrumentation 0/2/0/0 – 2/0/0/0 – str.

Catalogue of works

First performance Michala Petri/English Sinfonia/Steuart Bedford – Eye Parish Church, Suffolk, 3 June 1988 (Wingfield Arts & Music Concert)
First Europe performance Michala Petri/Slovak Chamber Orchestra – Tivoli Concert Hall, Copenhagen, Denmark, 7 July 1988
First broadcast performance Michala Petri/Scottish Chamber Orchestra/Jaime Laredo – Radio 3, 3 March 1990 (recorded in St Andrew's, Edinburgh, 27-28 October 1989)
First London performance Michala Petri/New London Orchestra/Ronald Corp – St John's Smith Square, London, 2 December 1995
Publisher Faber, 1992
Article Michala Petri, in 'Working with Malcolm Arnold' – *Maestro* 7, October 2020

Serenade for tenor and string orchestra ('Contrasts') Op.134 (1988)

[1. Hermit Hoar in Solemn Cell (Samuel Johnson) 2. Then tell me, what is the material world? (William Blake) 3. Saint Jerome in his Study kept a great big cat (Anon) 4. To this world farewell (Chikamatsu Monzaemon) 5. Answer July, where is the bee ...? (Emily Dickinson)
Words chosen by Robert Tear for whom it was written "with affection and admiration" and in celebration of Tear's 50th birthday – the work is dedicated to Anthony John Day
Duration 9'
First performance Robert Tear/City of London Sinfonia/Richard Hickox – St Andrew's Hall, Norwich, 11 April 1989
First performance (voice and piano) James Bowers (Ten.)/Alice Pinto (Pno.) – Royal & Derngate, Northampton, 17 October 2015 (Tenth Malcolm Arnold Festival)
Publisher Novello, 1989
Notes Originally Op.133 and entitled 'Robert's Contrasts'

Divertimento (Duo) for two B flat clarinets Op.135 (1988)

Duration 8'
First performance Patrick Saunders and James Aldous – Assembly Room, Hall for Cornwall, Truro, Cornwall, 2 October 1998 (Cornwall New Music Group Concert)
Publisher QTP

Concerto for cello and orchestra ('Shakespearean') Op.136 (1988 revised 2000)

Commissioned by the Royal Philharmonic Society, with additional funds provided by Greater London Arts as part of the Shakespearean festivities, and dedicated to Julian Lloyd Webber.
Duration 25' (21' – revised version)
Instrumentation 2+picc./2/2/2 – 4/3/3/1 – timp. perc. str.
Instr. (rev. version) 2/2/2/2 – 2/2/3/1 – timp.perc.str.
First performance Julian Lloyd Webber/Royal Philharmonic Orchestra/Vernon Handley – Royal Festival Hall, London, 9 March 1989 (Royal Philharmonic Society Concert)
First performance (revised version by David Ellis*) Stoian Razhkov/Musica Art Orchestra of Sofia/Martin Panteleev – St Markus Church, Schneppenbaum, Germany, 16 June 2003
First UK performance (revised version) Raphael Wallfisch/Northern Chamber Orchestra/ Nicholas Ward – Heritage Centre, Macclesfield, Cheshire, 12 February 2011
Publisher Novello, 1989

81

Notes *The revised version of the Concerto includes a cadenza by David Ellis.
Articles (i) David Ellis, 'Cello Concerto recording in preparation' – *Beckus* 78, Autumn 2010;
   Maestro 7, October 2020
(ii) Howard Sowerby, 'The Arnold Cello Concerto in concert' – *Beckus* 80, Spring 2011
(iii) Michael Jameson, 'A Concerto rediscovered: Sir Malcolm Arnold and the British cello
   concerto' – *Beckus* 92, Spring 2014

Wind Octet Op.137 (1988)
Commissioned by the Manchester Camerata Wind Soloists with financial assistance from
North West Arts and dedicated to Janet Hilton.
Duration 15'
Instrumentation 2Ob. 2Cl. 2Bsn. 2Hn.
First performance Manchester Camerata Wind Soloists/Janet Hilton – Royal Northern
   College of Music, Manchester, 17 February 1990
First London performance above artists – Wigmore Hall, London, 15 March 1990
First broadcast performance above artists – Radio 3, 15 April 1991
First Europe performance Student Wind Ensemble – Helsinki, Finland, 14 October 2014
Publisher Novello, 1989
Article Janet Hilton, 'Playing Malcolm's clarinet works' – *Beckus* 101, Summer 2016

Four Welsh Dances for orchestra Op.138 (1988)
Commissioned by the Hallé Concerts Society with funds provided by Bass North Ltd, and
dedicated to Emrys Lloyd-Roberts.
Duration 10'
Instrumentation 2+picc./2/2/2 – 4/3/3/1 – timp. perc.(2) hp. str.
First performance Hallé Orchestra/Owain Arwel Hughes – Free Trade Hall, Manchester, 19
   June 1989
First Wales performance above artists – St David's Hall, Cardiff, 21 July 1989 (Cardiff Prom)
First US performance North Carolina Symphony Orchestra/Grant Llewellyn – Mexmandi
   Concert Hall, North Carolina, 31 December 2007
Publisher Novello, 1989
Article Paul Jackson, 'Four Welsh Dances' (with music examples) – *Beckus* 6, October 1992;
   Maestro 1, October 2014

(a) Four Welsh Dances for wind band Op.138a (2003) arranged by Peter Parkes
First Europe performance Technical University of Braunschweig Orchestra/Markus Ludke –
   Technical University of Braunschweig, Braunschweig, Germany, 27 January 2019
Publisher Novello

Two Songs for voice and full orchestra [sketches] (1988-89)
[1. The Sheep Under the Snow 2. The Rival Cockade]
Notes Maybe rejected songs from 'Contrasts' Op.134

Violin Concerto Op.140 [sketches] (1988-89)
Written for Nigel Kennedy
Duration 20-23'
Instrumentation 2 + picc./2/2/2 – 4/3/3/1 – timp.perc.(2) str.
Notes (i) Op.140 was later allocated to the Fantasy for recorder and string quartet (1990)

(ii) sketches, begun on 22 November 1988, consist of an opening cadenza and over hundred bars in short score

Concerto for B flat soprano saxophone [sketches] (1989)
Instrumentation 1/1/2/2/ – 2/0/0/0 – str.

Flourish for a Battle, for wind band Op.139 (1989)
Commissioned by the Royal Air Force Benevolent Fund and dedicated to the RAF Benevolent Fund's 50th anniversary of the Battle of Britain Appeal.
Duration 10'
First performance Royal Air Force Band/Wing Cdr Barrie Hingley – Royal Festival Hall, London, 6 April 1990 (at a concert marking the 50th anniversary of the Battle of Britain, given in the presence of Her Majesty the Queen and HRH the Duke of Edinburgh)
Publisher Novello, 1990

(a) arranged for seven instruments by the composer (no date)
Instrumentation Alto Cl. Bs. Cl. Bar.Sax. Bsn.(2) Euph. Tba.

Theme and Variations: Fantasy for recorder and string quartet Op.140 (1990)
Commissioned for Michala Petri by the Carnegie Hall Corporation in honour of the Carnegie Hall's Centennial Season and dedicated to Michala Petri.
Duration 20'
First performance Michala Petri/Cavani String Quartet – Weill Recital Hall, Carnegie Hall, New York, 15 March 1991
First UK performance Evelyn Nallen/Lindsay String Quartet – Music Department, Manchester University, 15 November 1991 (Arnold/Haydn Celebration Concert series)
First London performance Michala Petri/members of the Academy of St Martin-in-the-Fields – Barbican Hall, London, 11 March 1992
Publisher Novello, 1991
Article Michala Petri, 'Working with Malcolm Arnold' – *Maestro* 7, October 2020

(a) arranged for recorder and string orchestra by Giles Easterbrook (1991 rev.2004)
First performance Michala Petri/Guildhall String Ensemble/Robert Salter – Royal Hall, Harrogate, Yorkshire, 6 August 1991 (Harrogate Festival)
First Europe performance Michala Petri/Irish Chamber Orchestra/James Galway – National Concert Hall, Dublin, 30 September 1991 (broadcast 'live' on RTE)
First London performance John Turner/Camerata Ensemble – St John's Smith Square, London, 16 April 2004*
Publisher Novello, as Theme and Variations for recorder and strings, Op.140a (1991)
Notes *This was also the first performance of the revised version by David Ellis

Robert Kett Overture for orchestra Op.141 (1990)
Commissioned by the Education Department of the Norfolk County Council.
Duration 8'
Instrumentation 2+picc./2/2/2 – 4/3/3/1 – timp. perc.(4) str.
First performance Norfolk County Youth Orchestra/Simon Halsey – St Andrew's Hall, Norwich, 25 July 1990 (Kings Lynn Festival)

First London performance Norwich Students' Orchestra – Royal Festival Hall, London, 13 July 1996 (National Festival of Music for Youth)

Publisher Novello, 1990

Notes Robert Kett, a local tanner and Norfolk landowner, was the leader of the 16th century rebellion, which first blockaded then took possession of Norwich, in protest against their eviction from the common land. Kett's Oak, from where the insurgents began their march to Norwich in 1549, can still be seen near Wymondham [the composer's former home].

A Manx Suite for orchestra (Little Suite No.3) Op.142 (1990)

Commissioned by Alan Pickard, Music Adviser, Isle of Man Department of Education for the Manx Youth Orchestra under the patronage of the Isle of Man Bank Ltd in celebration of the Bank's 125th anniversary.

Duration 10'

Instrumentation 2+picc./2/2/2 + cbsn. – 4/3/3/1 – timp. perc.(2) hp. str.

First performance Manx Youth Orchestra/Alan Pickard – Villa Marina, Douglas, Isle of Man, 8 December 1990.

Publisher Novello, 1990

Notes A number of Manx tunes are incorporated in the score.

Sinfonia Concertante for horn, viola and orchestra [sketches] Op.143 (1989-90)

Notes Discussions were already in hand as early as January 1989 for a London Festival Orchestra commission, specifically for a 15-minute work entitled Sinfonia Concertante for violin, cello, oboe, horn and strings, to be performed at Norwich Cathedral in July 1991. By February 1991 the composition had been renamed as above with a planned premiere for Arnold's 70th birthday concert at London's Queen Elizabeth Hall on 21 October 1991 performed by Ross Pople and the London Festival Orchestra.

A Flavour of Ischia for orchestra Op.144 (1990/91)

Duration c. 20'

Dedicated to the memory of Sir William Walton

Instrumentation 2+picc./2/2/2+cbsn. – 4/3/3/1 – timp.hp.cel. str

Notes Slated to be performed at the Barbican, London, on 18 July 1992 by the Incorporated Association of Preparatory Schools Orchestra conducted by Mark Lubbock

The Forces Fanfare for brass ensemble and percussion (1991)

Commissioned by the USAF Band

Duration 3'

Instrumentation Hn.(6), Tpt.(6), Tbn.(6), Tba.(2) – timp.perc.(4/5)

First performance USAF Band/Lt Col Alan L Bonner – Constitution Hall, Washington DC, USA, 14 September 1991

Publisher Faber. 1999

Notes (i) the first British performance was originally planned for 22 July 1998 at the Royal Military School of Music, Kneller Hall, Twickenham, Middlesex.

(ii) The Fanfare incorporates parts of the Farnham Festival Fanfare and the motif from the last movement of Symphony No.6

Publisher Faber

Bolivar: music for orchestra (c.2004) arranged/edited by David Ellis
Duration 5-6'
Instrumentation 2+picc./2/2/2 – 4/3/3/1 – timp.perc.hp.str
Notes Originally intended for the opening titles of a Venezuelan film on the life of Simon Bolivar, it has two versions: one with a concert ending and the other with an optional 'fade'.

Fantasy for double bass (no date)
Duration 7'
First performance Alice Kent – Royal & Derngate, Northampton, 15 October 2015 (Tenth Malcolm Arnold Festival)
Publisher QTP
Notes Completed from a handful of sketches by Matthew Taylor
Article Leon Bosch, 'Fantasy for double bass' – *Beckus* 107, Winter 2017

Fanfare for three trumpets (no date)
Incomplete sketch

Appendix A. Ballet music

Ballets with purposely-written music
(see main catalogue)

- Homage to the Queen Op.42 (1952)
- Rinaldo and Armida Op.49 (1954)
- Solitaire (1956) [uses the English Dances – see table on page 89]
- Sweeney Todd Op.68 (1959)
- Elektra Op.79 (1963)

Ballets based on one piece of music
(see under original work in main catalogue)[1]

- Journey (1979) – Organ Concerto
- Bertram Batell's Sideshow (1970) – Toy Symphony
- Hands (1975) – Concerto for Two Pianos (3 Hands) (2nd movt)
- Flowers of the Forest (1985) – Four Scottish Dances
- Alice in Wonderland (1993) – Four Irish Dances
- Three Fantasies (1995) – Three Fantasies for Piano
- *Untitled* (2002) – The Fair Field Overture
- *Untitled* (2006) – Clarinet Concerto No.2
- 25 (2012) – Concerto for Two Pianos (3 Hands) (2nd and 3rd movts)
- Suite Bourgeoise (2014) – Suite Bourgeoise
- MA Serenade (2014) – Serenade for Small Orchestra
- Grand Fantasia Op 973 (2015) – Grand Fantasia
- Generation Y (2016) – Symphony No.5
- Concerto for Joyce and Dennis (2017) – Concerto for Two Pianos (3 Hands)

---

1   The following ballet requires further research: an untitled ballet was performed by the American Dance Theatre in San Mateo, California, in March 1977. The music included Debussy's *March Ecossaise* and four of Arnold's *English Dances* – choreographer: unknown.

Dallcts which uce multiple pieces of music

(see table on page 89)[2]

- Scottish Suite (Highland Fair) (1961)
- Peter Pan (1993)
- Alice, Dreams and Wonderland (1998)
- Peter Pan (2000)
- Peter Pan (2002)
- The Three Musketeers (2006)
- Peter Pan (2014)

Further details of composite ballets

Scottish Suite (1961)
Choreographer: Walter Goehr
First performance London Ballet Company – Hintlesham Hall, Nr Ipswich, 28 August 1961
    (Hintlesham Festival)

later re-created as Highland Fair (1965)
Choreographer: Michael Smuin
First performance Harkness Ballet Company – in the East Room of The White House,
    Washington DC, 29 September 1965 (in the presence of President Lyndon B Johnson)

Peter Pan (1993)
Choreography: Anna du Boisson
First performance West London School of Dance – Commonwealth Institute, Holland Park,
    London, June 1994 (subsequent performances in 2007, 2011 and 2013 have all been held
    at the Bloomsbury Theatre in London's West End)
Article Alan Poulton, 'Peter Pan' – *Beckus* 98, Autumn 2015

Alice, Dreams and Wonderland (1998)
Choreographer: Alexander Roy
Associate Director: Christina Gallea
First performance Alexander Roy London Ballet Theatre Company – Camberley Arts Link,
    Surrey, 2 October 1998 (followed by an extensive tour of the UK and Europe between
    October and December 1998)
Notes The music of Ligeti is also used in some of the scenes

Peter Pan (2000)
Choreographer: Alun Jones
Artistic Director: Helen Starr
First performance Louisville Ballet – Whitney Hall, Kentucky Centre for the Arts, Louisville,
    Kentucky, USA, 24 February 2000

---

2   More detailed information on these composite ballets can be found in the Malcolm
Arnold Society annual journal *Maestro*, particularly issue no.4, October 2017, as well as
the quarterly newsletter *Beckus*.

Peter Pan (2002)

Choreographer: Kathi Ferguson
First performance Howard County Ballet – John Rouse Theatre, Wilde Lake High School,
  Columbia, Maryland, USA, May 2002
Notes An all-Arnold score (no further details available despite several written enquiries)

The Three Musketeers (2006)

Duration 135'
Choreographer: David Nixon
Music arranged/orchestrated by John Longstaff
Instrumentation 2/1/2/1 – 2/2/1/0 – timp.perc.pno.(cel.)hp. str.
First performance Northern Ballet/John Pryce-Jones – Alhambra Theatre, Bradford, 23
  September 2006
First London performance Northern Ballet – Sadler's Wells Theatre, London, 16 May 2007
First Europe performance Estonian National Ballet Company – Tallinn Opera House, Estonia,
  23 April 2008
First Canada performance Alberta Ballet Company/Calgary Philharmonic Orchestra/Peter
  Dala – Jubilee Theatre, Calgary, 23 October 2014
Articles/reviews: (i) Anthony Meredith, 'The Three Musketeers – a new Malcolm Arnold
  ballet' – *Beckus* 61, Summer 2006; *Maestro* 6, October 2019
(ii) Anthony Meredith, 'The Three Musketeers' – *Beckus* 68, Spring 2008
(iii) Adrian Harris, 'The Three Musketeers in Canada' – *Beckus* 95, Winter 2014
(iv) Anthony Meredith, 'Malcolm's Musketeers' – *Maestro* 2, October 2015
(iv) Adrian Harris, 'The return of The Three Musketeers' – *Beckus* 112, Spring 2019

Peter Pan (2014)

Choreographer: Steve McMahon
First performance Memphis Ballet – The Orpheum, Memphis, Tennessee, USA, April 2014
Notes Music by Carl Nielsen and William Walton is also used in the ballet.

	Solitaire	Scottish Suite	Peter Pan	Alice, Dreams and Wonderland	Peter Pan	The Three Musketeers	Peter Pan
	1956	1961	1994	1998	2000	2006	2014
Phantasy for string quartet (1941)						●	
Three Shanties Op.4					●		
Trio for flute viola and bassoon Op.6				●			
Flute sonatina Op.19				●			
Serenade Op.26				●		●	●
English Dances set 1 Op.27	●	●	●		●		●
Oboe concertino Op.28a				●			
Clarinet sonatina Op.29				●			
Concerto for piano duet Op.32				●			
English Dances set 2 Op.33	●	●	●		●	●	
Sound Barrier rhapsody Op.38					●		
Oboe concerto Op.39				●			
Symphony No.2 Op.40			●			●	
Flute concerto no.1 Op.45			●	●		●	
Sinfonietta No.1 Op.48			●			●	●
Sarabande and Polka (1956)	●		●		●		●
Scottish Dances Op.59		●	●		●		●
Duke of Cambridge March Op.60					●		
Symphony No.3 Op.63					●		
Sinfonietta No.2 Op.65			●				
Carnival of Animals Op.72			●				
Symphony No.5 Op.74					●		
Attleborough Suite Op.78a			●				
Little Suite Op.80							●
Sinfonietta No.3 Op.81			●	●			
Fantasy for oboe Op.90				●			
Cornish Dances Op.91			●		●	●	●
Anniversary Overture Op.99						●	●
Flute concerto no.2 Op.111					●		
Clarinet concerto no.2 Op.115			●				
Flute sonata Op.121						●	
Irish Dances Op.126			●			●	●
Fantasy for cello Op.130			●				
Welsh Dances Op.138					●		
Hobson's Choice (1953)			●			●	●
You Know What Sailors Are (1953)			●				
Trapeze (1956)					●		
Bridge on the River Kwai (1957)					●		
Roots of Heaven (1958)						●	
Inn of the Sixth Happiness (1958)					●		
No Love for Johnnie (1960)			●			●	
Whistle Down the wind (1961)					●		
David Copperfield (1969)			●			●	

Appendix B. Film music arranged for concert performance (selective list)

Stolen Face (1952)

Ballade for piano and orchestra arranged by Philip Lane (1999)
Duration 9'
Instrumentation 2/2/2/2 – 4/3/3/0 – timp.perc.(2) hp.str.
First performance Sorina Aust-Ioan (Pno.)/Cologne Philharmonic Orchestra/Scott Lawton –
   Cologne Philharmonic Hall, Cologne, Germany, 15 October 2002
First UK concert performance Dominic Piers-Smith (Pno.)/Worthing Symphony Orchestra/
   John Gibbons – Royal & Derngate, Northampton, 17 October 2010 (Fifth Malcolm Arnold
   Festival)
First US performance soloist/Jefferson City Symphony Orchestra/Keith Clark – Jefferson City,
   9 February 2016
Publisher Novello
Articles (i) Phillip Dyson, 'Ballade of the Stolen Face' – *Beckus* 39, Winter 2000; *Maestro* 3,
   October 2016
(ii) Alan Poulton, 'Bronwen Jones: pianist in Stolen Face' – *Beckus* 105, Summer 2017
(iii) Adrian Harris, 'Susquehanna Symphony Orchestra' – *Beckus* 106, Autumn 2017
(iv) Phillip Dyson, 'Malcolm's piano music' – *Beckus* 108, Spring 2018

The Holly and the Ivy (1952)

Suite for orchestra arranged by Christopher Palmer (1991)
Duration 6'
Instrumentation 3/2/2/2 – 4/3/3/1 – timp. perc.(3) (cel.) hp.(2) str.
First performance London Symphony Orchestra/Richard Hickox – Barbican Hall, London, 21
   December 1991 (LSO Christmas Concert)
First Canada performance Fremont Symphony Orchestra – Fremont, 10 December 1993
First US performance Boston Pops Esplanade Orchestra/Keith Lockhart – Symphony Hall,
   Boston, 10 December 1999
First Japan performance Student Orchestra of Sensoku College of Music – Senozu Gakuen
   Maeda Hall, 18 December 2001
First Europe performance RTE Concert Orchestra/Gareth Hudson – The Helix, Dublin, Ireland,
   7 December 2002
Publisher Novello (study score)
Notes Subtitled 'A Fantasy on Christmas Carols' the music is derived from the film's
   soundtrack and the 1957 television documentary 'Christmas Around the World', as well

Appendix B. Film music arranged for concert performance (selective list)

as the carol arrangements Arnold made for the 'Save the Children' fund in 1960 – see also Appendix E.

You Know What Sailors Are (1953)

Excerpt 'Scherzetto' arranged for clarinet* and small orchestra by Christopher Palmer
    (c.1991)
Duration 2'30"
Instrumentation 1/1/0/0 – 4/0/0/0 – perc.(2) cel. hp. str
First performance John Bradbury (Cl.)/BBC Philharmonic Orchestra/Rumon Gamba (Chandos
    CD recording, New Broadcasting House, Manchester, February and July 2000)
First concert performance Catherine Ruckwardt (Cl.)/Philharmonie State Orchestra – Mainz,
    Germany, 1 April 2008 (the concert was repeated the following day)
First British concert performance Emma Dyer (Cl.)/Northamptonshire County Youth
    Orchestra/Tim Green – Royal & Derngate, Northampton, 17 October 2010 (Fifth Malcolm
    Arnold Festival)
Publisher Novello (orchestral version); QTP, 2001 (version for clarinet and piano)
Notes *Played by Frederick Thurston on the film's soundtrack

Hobson's Choice (1953)

(a) 'Selections' from the film arranged for small orchestra by Tony Fones (1954)
Duration 7'
Instrumentation 1+picc./1/2/1 – 2/3/2/0 – timp.perc.hp. str
Publisher Paterson (piano conductor)

(b) Concert Suite from the film arranged for orchestra by Christopher Palmer (1992)
Duration 17'
Instrumentation 2/2/2/2 – 4/2/2/1 – timp. perc.(3) pno. (cel.) hp. str
First performance Wren Orchestra/Iain Sutherland – Kenwood House, London, 1 July 1995
First amateur performance Rochdale Youth Orchestra/John Binns – Gracie Fields Theatre,
    Rochdale, 8 July 1995 (concert given in the presence of the composer)
First Europe performance Cologne Philharmonic Orchestra/Scott Lawton – Cologne
    Philharmonic Hall, Cologne, Germany, 15 October 2002
Publisher Novello (study score)

(c) Suite arranged for piano trio by the Canadian pianist, Leslie Hogan (1994)
Duration 12'
Instrumentation Vn. Vc. Pno.
First UK performance Paul Manley (Vn.)/Judith Herbert (Vc.)/Diana Ambache (Pno.) –
    Shakespeare Institute, Stratford-upon-Avon, 21 October 2001 (Malcolm Arnold's 80th
    birthday party held in conjunction with the Sixth English Music Festival)
First London performance Marcia Crayford (Vn.)/Paul Watkins (Vc.)/Richard Shaw (Pno.) –
    Wigmore Hall, London, 23 October 2001 (80th Birthday Concert)
Publisher QTP, 1995

(d) Suite: 'Hobson's Choice' arranged for brass band by Robin Dewhurst, Peter Graham
    and Derek Scott (1996)
Duration 17'

First performance University of Salford Brass Band/David King – Peel Hall, University of
   Salford, 6 November 1996
Notes The score was presented to Sir Malcolm Arnold to commemorate his visit to the
   University of Salford
Unpublished

(e) Suite: 'Hobson's Brass' arranged for brass band by Phillip Littlemore (2007)
Duration 10'
First performance Rushden Town Band/Adele Hudson – Royal & Derngate, Northampton, 14
   October 2018 (Thirteenth Malcolm Arnold Festival)
Publisher Faber

(f) 'Hobson's' for wind octet – themes from the film arranged by Uwe Radok (2006)
Publisher QTP, 2006

The Captain's Paradise (1953)

**'Postcard from the Med' – excerpt from the film, re-constructed, arranged and
   orchestrated by Philip Lane (c.1999)**
Duration 4'
Instrumentation 2/2/2+ten.sax/2 – 4/3/4/1 – timp.perc.(4) pno.hp.egtr. str.
First performance BBC Philharmonic Orchestra/Rumon Gamba (Chandos CD recording, New
   Broadcasting House, Manchester, February and July 2000)
First concert performance Philharmonie State Orchestra – Mainz, Germany, 1 April 2008 (the
   concert was repeated the following day)
Publisher Novello

The Belles of St Trinian's (1954)

**Comedy Suite: 'Exploits for Orchestra' arranged by Christopher Palmer (1988) and edited
   by Philip Lane (1999)**
Duration 8'
Instrumentation 2/1/2/1 – 0/2/1/1 – perc.(4) pno.duet, str
First performance Paul Janes (Pno.)/BBC Philharmonic Orchestra/Rumon Gamba (Chandos
   CD recording, New Broadcasting House, Manchester, February and July 2000)
First televised performance Roderick Elms and Alistair Young/BBC Concert Orchestra/Rumon
   Gamba – BBC Television, 16 August 2003 (Promenade Concert from the Royal Albert
   Hall, London)
First Europe performance Cologne Philharmonic Orchestra/Scott Lawton – Cologne
   Philharmonic Hall, Cologne, Germany, 15 October 2002
Publisher Novello

Trapeze (1956)

Suite from the film, reconstructed, arranged and orchestrated by Philip Lane (1999)
Duration 13'30"
Instrumentation 2/2/2/2 – 4/3/3/1 – timp.perc.(3) hp.acc.str.
First performance BBC Philharmonic Orchestra/Rumon Gamba (Chandos CD recording, New
   Broadcasting House, Manchester, February and July 2000)

First concert performance (Overture only) Malcolm Arnold Festival Orchestra/John Gibbons
– Royal & Derngate, Northampton, 17 October 2010 (Fifth Malcolm Arnold Festival)
First concert performance (complete) Northamptonshire County Youth Orchestra/Chris
Hiscock – Malcolm Arnold Academy, Northampton, 13 October 2019 (Fourteenth
Malcolm Arnold Festival)
Publisher Novello

The Bridge on the River Kwai (1957)

(a) Suite from the film arranged for large orchestra by Christopher Palmer (1991)
Commissioned by the BBC in honour of Malcolm Arnold's 80th birthday
Duration 29'
Instrumentation 3/3/3+eflat cl./2+cbsn. – 4/3/3/1 – timp. perc.(6) pno.(2) hp.(2) str
First performance BBC Concert Orchestra/Barry Wordsworth – Queen Elizabeth Hall,
London, 26 October 1991 (Malcolm Arnold 70th Birthday Concert)
First Europe performance National Symphony Orchestra of Ireland – National Concert Hall,
Dublin, 8 July 1994
First US performance (Excerpts) Susquehanna Symphony Orchestra/Sheldon Bair – John
Carroll School, Bel Air, Maryland, 11 March 2000
First Australia performance Queensland Symphony Orchestra/Guy Noble – Queensland
Performing Arts Centre, Brisbane, 22 October 2017
Publisher Novello

(b) above suite transcribed for wind band by Yoshihiro Kimura
First performance Hiroshima Wind Orchestra/Yoshihiro Kimura

(c) Excerpt 'The River Kwai March' arranged for wind band by Eric Osterling (1958)
Duration 4'
Publisher Shapiro, Bernstein & Co Inc

(d) Excerpt 'The River Kwai March' arranged for junior wind band by John Higgins (1998)
Publisher Hal Leonard, in 'The Big Picture – Epic Movie Themes'

Notes For other arrangements of the 'River Kwai March' see *Maestro* 7, October 2020

The Roots of Heaven (1958)

(a) Overture – reconstructed from the parts in 1983
Written at the request of Darryl F Zanuck, the film's producer, for the US premiere in
October 1958 (see *Maestro* 7, October 2019)
Duration 5'15"
Instrumentation 2/2/2/1+cbsn. – 4/3/3/1 – timp.perc.(2) pno. (cel.) hp. str.
First UK concert performance BBC Concert Orchestra/Carl Davis – Radio 3, 21 March 1995
('Music for the British Movies' series)
First US concert performance Peninsular Symphony Orchestra/Mitchell Sardou Klein – San
Mateo, California, 18 January 2008
Publisher Novello

(b) Overture also arranged for brass band (and wind band) by Neil Richmond (2002)
First performance (brass band version) Harrogate Band/Neil Richmond – Starbeck Chapel, Harrogate, 17 May 2003
Article Neil Richmond, 'Transcribing Arnold's works' – *Beckus* 108, Spring 2018
Unpublished

The Inn of the Sixth Happiness (1958)

(a) Selection arranged for brass band by Edrich Siebert (1961)
Duration 6'
Publisher B. Feldman; Studio Music

(b) Suite from the film arranged for orchestra by Christopher Palmer (1992)
Duration 14'
Instrumentation 3/2/3/2 – 4/3/3/1 – timp.perc.(4) pno. (cel.) hp.(2) str
First performance Hampshire County Youth Orchestra – Bryanston School, Blandford, Dorset, 11 April 1993
First professional performance Bournemouth Symphony Orchestra/Richard Hickox – Wessex Hall, Poole, Dorset, 18 September 1993
First London performance Royal Academy of Music Sinfonia/Ron Goodwin – Duke's Hall, Royal Academy of Music, London, 18 June 1996 (British and American Film Music Festival)
First Europe performance Cologne Philharmonic Orchestra/Scott Lawton – Cologne Philharmonic Hall, Cologne, Germany 15 October 2002
First Japan performance Student Orchestra – College Hall, Tanagawa, 8 March 2003
First US performance Grant Park Festival – Chicago, Illinois, 31 July 2004
Publisher EMI/Novello (study score), 1992

(c) 'Inn that Brings the Sixth Happiness' – above suite, transcribed for symphonic wind band by Munetoshi Senoo (1996)
Publisher Novello; EMI Music Pub (Japan), 1996

The Boy and the Bridge (1959)

Overture (Allegro and March) arranged for small orchestra, probably by Tony Fones (c.1959)
Duration 3'30"
Instrumentation 2+picc.1/2/1 – 2/2/3/0 – perc.hp.cel.str.
First concert performance Malcolm Arnold Festival Orchestra/John Gibbons – Royal & Derngate, Northampton, 17 October 2010 (Fifth Malcolm Arnold Festival)
Publisher B. Feldman & Co (piano conductor)

No Love for Johnnie (1960)

Suite from the film reconstructed and orchestrated by Philip Lane
Duration 10'30"
Instrumentation 2/2/2/2 – 4/2/3/1 – timp. perc.(3) cel. hp. str.
First performance BBC Philharmonic Orchestra/Rumon Gamba (Chandos CD recording, New Broadcasting House, Manchester, February and July 2000)

First concert performance Malcolm Arnold Festival Orchestra/John Gibbons – Royal &
    Derngate, Northampton, 17 October 2010 (Fifth Malcolm Arnold Festival)
Publisher Novello
Notes Malcolm Arnold conducted the London Symphony Orchestra in his own Suite from
    the film which was broadcast on the Light Programme, 9 August 1961

Whistle Down the Wind (1961)

Suite from the film arranged for small orchestra by Christopher Palmer (1991)
Duration 9'
Instrumentation 2/1/2/0 – 2/0/0/0 – perc.(2) pno. (cel.) gtr. hp. str. (max. 8/6/4/4/2)
First performance Perth Youth Orchestra – Perth City Hall, Scotland, 11 April 1993
First professional performance London Symphony Orchestra/Richard Hickox – Barbican Hall,
    London, 16 December 1993 (LSO Christmas Concert)
Publisher Novello

Tamahine (1963)

Excerpt direct from the film, 'Royal Fireworks Music', for wind band
First concert performance Royal Northern College of Music Wind Ensemble/Clark Rundell –
    Royal Northern College of Music, Manchester, 3 November 1984 (BASWBE Conference)
Unpublished

The Heroes of Telemark (1965)

Suite from the film arranged for orchestra by John Gibbons (2017)
Duration c.10'
First performance Royal Philharmonic Orchestra/John Gibbons – Royal & Derngate,
    Northampton, 15 October 2017 (Twelfth Malcolm Arnold Festival)
Unpublished

David Copperfield (1969)

Suite from the film arranged for orchestra by Philip Lane (1999)
Duration 11"
Instrumentation 2/2/2/2 – 4/2/3/1 – perc.(2/3) cel. hp.str.
First performance Kensington Symphony Orchestra/Russell Keable – Queen Elizabeth Hall,
    London, 21 January 2003
First US performance Susquehanna Symphony Orchestra/Sheldon Bair – Abingdon,
    Maryland, 16 May 2009
First Australia performance Heidelberg Symphony Orchestra/Christopher Kopke – Ivanhoe
    Girls' Grammar School, Melbourne, Victoria, 1 April 2017
Publisher Novello

Appendix C. List of feature films

See also: 'Arnold's published film music' (*Maestro* 3); 'Arnold film and concert music on 7"vinyl' (*Maestro* 4); 'Arnold's feature films and their literary sources' (*Maestro* 6); 'Feature Films in Performance' (includes CDs and DVDs) (*Maestro* 7).

Badger's Green (1948)
Highbury Productions
Producer John Croydon and Adrian Worker
Director John Irwin
Music played by London Symphony Orchestra/John Hollingsworth
Articles (i) Graham Escott, 'The Road to Badger's Green' – *Beckus* 72, Spring 2009
(ii) Alan Poulton, 'Badger's Green: Arnold's first film score' – *Beckus* 111, Winter 2018

Britannia Mews (1949)
Twentieth Century Fox Productions
US title The Forbidden Street
Alt title The Affairs of Adelaide
Producer William Perlberg
Director Jean Negulesco
Music played by Royal Philharmonic Orchestra/Muir Mathieson

Your Witness (1949)
Coronado Productions
US title Eye Witness
Producer Joan Harrison
Director Robert Montgomery
Music played by London Symphony Orchestra/John Hollingsworth

The Astonished Heart (1949) [arranger/uncredited]
Gainsborough Pictures/Sidney Box
Producer Anthony Darnborough
Director Terence Fisher
Music played by London Symphony Orchestra/Muir Mathieson
Notes William Blezard was asked to provide special arrangements of Noel Coward's music and, owing to the very tight deadlines required by the Director and Producer, Malcolm Arnold volunteered to assist him with the final orchestrations; their joint contribution to the film's soundtrack was uncredited.

Up for the Cup (1950) [part/uncredited]
Henry Halstead Productions (Byron Films)

Appendix C. List of feature films

Producer Henry Halstead and Alan Cullimore
Director Jack Raymond
Notes Percival Mackey composed most of the music, but Malcolm Arnold scored several of
the longer sequences (uncredited).

No Highway (1950)
Twentieth Century-Fox
Producer Louis D Lighton
Director Henry Koster
US title No Highway in the Sky
Music played by Orchestra/Marcus Dods
Notes No incidental music: only title and end-title music employed.

Home to Danger (1950)
New World Pictures/Eros Films
Producer Lance Comfort
Director Terence Fisher
Music played by Royal Philharmonic Orchestra/Muir Mathieson

Wings of Danger (1950)
Hammer Films
Producer Anthony Hinds
Director Terence Fisher
US title Dead on Course
Music played by London Philharmonic Orchestra/Malcolm Arnold

Home at Seven (1950)
London Film Productions
Producer Maurice Cowan
Director Ralph Richardson
US title Murder on Monday
Music played by Royal Philharmonic Orchestra/Muir Mathieson

Stolen Face (1952)
Hammer Films
Producer Anthony Hinds
Director Terence Fisher
Music played by Bronwen Jones (piano)/London Philharmonic Orchestra/Malcolm Arnold
Notes Music from the film was arranged as 'Ballade for piano and orchestra' by Philip Lane
(1999) – see Appendix B.
Article Alan Poulton: 'Bronwen Jones – pianist in Stolen Face' – *Beckus* 105, Summer 2017

The Holly and the Ivy (1952)
London Film Productions
Producer Anatole de Grunwald
Director George More O'Ferrall
Music played by Royal Philharmonic Orchestra/Muir Mathieson
Notes (i) The soundtrack includes the traditional Christmas carol 'The Holly and the Ivy',

97

originally published by Cecil Sharp and in an arrangement by H Walford Davis.

(ii) Music from the film, together with other Arnold carol arrangements, was arranged as a suite subtitled 'A Fantasy on Christmas Carols' by Christopher Palmer (1991) – see Appendix B.

The Sound Barrier (1952)
London Film Productions
Producer/Director David Lean
US title Breaking (Through) the Sound Barrier
Music played by Royal Philharmonic Orchestra/Muir Mathieson
Notes Arnold produced his orchestral rhapsody 'The Sound Barrier' Op.38 (q.v.), based on the main themes from the film, whose development follows the story line of the film.
Article Christopher Ritchie, 'The Arnold-Lean Trilogy, Part 1' – *Beckus* 27, Winter 1997 and *Maestro* 1, October 2014

Curtain Up (1952)
Constellation Films
Producer Robert Garrett
Director Ralph Smart
Music played by Royal Philharmonic Orchestra/Muir Mathieson

The Ringer (1952)
London Film Productions
Producer Hugh Perceval
Director Guy Hamilton
Alt title The Gaunt Stranger
Music played by Royal Philharmonic Orchestra/Muir Mathieson

It Started in Paradise (1952)
British Film-Makers
Producers Sergei Nolbandov and Leslie Parkyn
Director Compton Bennett
Alt title Fanfare for Figleaves
Music played by Royal Philharmonic Orchestra/Muir Mathieson

Four Sided Triangle (1952)
Hammer Films
Producers Michael Carreras and Alexander Paal
Director Terence Fisher
Alt title The Monster and the Woman
Music played by Royal Philharmonic Orchestra/Muir Mathieson
Notes The soundtrack includes Mendelssohn's 'Wedding March' arranged by Malcolm Arnold.

Invitation to the Dance (1952) [rejected]
MGM
Director/Choreographer Gene Kelly
Music played by Royal Philharmonic Orchestra/John Hollingsworth

Notes This balletic film is in three parts: 1. 'Circus', with music composed by Jacques Ibert; 2. 'Ring Around the Rosy', with music composed by André Previn; 3. 'Sinbad the Sailor', with music adapted from Rimsky-Korsakov's *Sheherazade*.
Arnold provided a 20-minute ballet score for 'Ring Around the Rosy', the second part of the film, but Gene Kelly and his producers were apparently dissatisfied with the music and it was rejected. André Previn was brought in to provide an alternative score which had to exactly match Kelly's original choreography to Arnold's now-rejected music!
Article Alan Poulton, 'Invitation to the Dance' – *Maestro* 4, October 2017

Devil on Horseback (1953)
Group 3
Producer John Grierson
Director Cyril Frankel
Alt title The Boy Jockey
Music played by Orchestra/Malcolm Arnold

The Story of Gilbert and Sullivan (1953) [arranger/uncredited]
London Film Productions
Directors/Producers Sidney Gilliat/Leslie Gilliat/Frank Launder
Alt title Gilbert and Sullivan
US title The Great Gilbert and Sullivan
Music played by London Symphony Orchestra/Sir Malcolm Sargent, with the D'Oyly Carte Opera Company Chorus and soloists
Notes Muir Mathieson appeared as the on-screen conductor and Malcolm Arnold was the uncredited music arranger.

The Captain's Paradise (1953)
London Film Productions
Director/Producer Anthony Kimmins
Original title Paradise
Alt title The Captain's Progress
Music played by Orchestra/Muir Mathieson
Notes Music from the film was arranged as 'Postcard from the Med' by Philip Lane (c.1999) – see Appendix B.

Albert R.N. (1953)
Angel Productions
Producer Daniel M Angel
Director Lewis Gilbert
Alt title Spare Man
US title Break to Freedom
US Alt title Marlag 'O' Prison Camp
Music played by Orchestra/Philip Martell

You Know What Sailors Are (1953)
Group Film Productions
Producers Peter Rogers and Julian Wintle
Director Ken Annakin

Music played by Orchestra/Muir Mathieson
Notes Music from the film was arranged as 'Scherzetto for clarinet and small orchestra' by
Christopher Palmer (c.1991) – see Appendix B.

Hobson's Choice (1953)
London Film Productions
Producer/Director David Lean
Music played by Royal Philharmonic Orchestra/Muir Mathieson
Notes Several arrangements of music from the film have been made for various forces:
orchestra, brass band, and chamber groups – see Appendix B.
Article Christopher Ritchie, 'The Arnold-Lean Trilogy, Part 2' – *Beckus* 28, Spring 1998 &
Maestro 1, October 2014

The Sleeping Tiger (1954)
Victor Hanbury Productions (Insignia Films)
Producer Victor Hanbury (aka Joseph Losey)
Director Joseph Losey
Music played by Orchestra/Muir Mathieson

Beautiful Stranger (1954)
Marksman Productions
Producers Maxwell Setton and John R Sloan
Director David Miller
US title Twist of Fate
Music played by Orchestra/Malcolm Arnold

The Belles of St Trinian's (1954)
London Film Productions
Producers Sidney Gilliat and Frank Launder
Director Frank Launder
Music played by Orchestra/Malcolm Arnold
Notes Music from the film was arranged as Comedy Suite: 'Exploits for Orchestra' by
Christopher Palmer (1988) and edited by Philip Lane (1999) – see Appendix B.

The Sea shall not have them (1954)
Angel Productions
Producer Daniel M Angel
Director Lewis Gilbert
Music played by London Philharmonic Orchestra/Muir Mathieson

The Constant Husband (1954)
Individual Pictures
Producers Sidney Gilliat and Frank Launder
Director Sidney Gilliat
Alt title Marriage à la Mode
Music played by London Philharmonic Orchestra/Muir Mathieson

A Prize of Gold (1954)
Warwick Film Productions
Producer Phil C Samuel
Director Mark Robson
Music played by London Symphony Orchestra/Muir Mathieson

The Night my Number came up (1955)
Ealing Studios/Michael Balcon Productions
Producer Michael Balcon
Director Leslie Norman
Music played by London Symphony Orchestra/Muir Mathieson

I am a Camera (1955)
Romulus
Producer John Woolf
Director Henry Cornelius
Music played by Orchestra/Muir Mathieson

Value for Money (1955)
Group Film Productions
Producer Sergei Nolbandov
Director Ken Annakin
Music played by Orchestra/Muir Mathieson
Notes The Hanwell Silver Band appear in the opening 'funeral sequence'.

The Deep Blue Sea (1955)
London Film Productions
Producer Alexander Korda
Director Anatole Litvak
Music played by Orchestra/Muir Mathieson

The Woman for Joe (1955)
Group Film Productions
Producer Leslie Parkyn
Director George More O'Ferrall
Music played by Orchestra/Muir Mathieson

1984 (1955)
Holiday Film Productions
Producer N Peter Rathvon
Director Michael Anderson
Music played by London Symphony Orchestra/Louis Levy

Port Afrique (1956)
Coronado Productions
Producers David E Rose and John R Sloan
Director Rudolph Maté
Music played by Orchestra/Muir Mathieson

Trapeze (1956)
Hill-Hecht-Lancaster-Productions
Producer James Hill
Director Carol Reed
Music played by Orchestra/Muir Mathieson
Notes Music from the film was arranged as a concert suite by Philip Lane (1999) – see Appendix B.

A Hill in Korea (1956)
Wessex Films
Producer Anthony Squire
Director Julian Amyes
US title Hell in Korea
Music played by Royal Philharmonic Orchestra/Muir Mathieson

Wicked as They Come (1956)
Frankovitch Productions (Film Locations)
UK Original title Portrait in Smoke
Producers Maxwell Setton and M J Frankovitch
Director Ken Hughes
Music played by Sinfonia of London/Muir Mathieson

The Barretts of Wimpole Street (1956) [rejected]
MGM British Studios
Producer Sam Zimbalist
Director Sidney Franklin
Notes Arnold composed and conducted the music for this film. However, Bronislau Kaper's music was eventually used when the film was released. There is no trace of Arnold's score, despite several enquiries.

Tiger in the Smoke (1956)
Rank Organisation
Producer Leslie Parkyn
Director Roy Ward Baker
Music played by Orchestra/Malcolm Arnold

Island in the Sun (1957)
Daryl F Zanuck Productions for Twentieth Century Fox
Producer Darryl F Zanuck
Director Robert Rossen
Music played by Royal Philharmonic Orchestra/Malcolm Arnold

Blue Murder at St Trinian's (1957)
John Harvel Productions
Producers Sidney Gilliat and Frank Launder
Director Frank Launder
Music played by Orchestra/Malcolm Arnold

Appendix C. List of feature films

The Bridge on the River Kwai (1957)
Horizon
Producer Sam Spiegel
Director David Lean
Music played by Royal Philharmonic Orchestra/Malcolm Arnold (recorded at Shepperton Studios, 21 October 1957 – Arnold's 36th birthday)
Notes (i) Arnold was awarded an Oscar for 'Best Music, Scoring' in 1958. He was not present at the ceremony and Morris Stoloff accepted the award on his behalf; the composer later collected his Oscar from Heathrow Airport after it had been cleared through customs.
(ii) In the opening scene, the prisoners march into the prison camp whistling 'Colonel Bogey', a First World War march written by F J Ricketts (aka Kenneth Alford); Arnold's River Kwai march, written as a counter-melody to 'Colonel Bogey', then fades in and takes over.
(iii) Music from the film was arranged as a suite for orchestra by Christopher Palmer (1991), as well as arrangements for wind band – see Appendix B.
Articles (i) Christopher Ritchie, 'The Arnold-Lean Trilogy, Part 3' – *Beckus* 30, Autumn 1998 & *Maestro* 1, October 2014
(ii) Alan Poulton, 'Kwai – a cinematic review' – *Maestro* 2, October 2015
(iii) David Dunstan, 'The Colonel Bogey saga' – *Beckus* 118, Autumn 2020

Dunkirk (1957)
Ealing Studios
Producer Michael Balcon
Director Leslie Norman
Music played by Sinfonia of London/Muir Mathieson

The Key (1958)
Open Road Films/Highwood Productions
Producer Carl Foreman
US Alt title Stella
Director Carol Reed
Music played by Orchestra/Malcolm Arnold

The Roots of Heaven (1958)
Darryl F Zanuck Productions for Twentieth Century Fox
Producer Darryl F Zanuck
Director John Huston
Music played by [London] Royal Philharmonic Orchestra/Malcolm Arnold
Notes The Overture from the film was reconstructed for orchestra (1983), and subsequently arranged for brass band (and wind band) by Neil Richmond (2002) – see Appendix B.

The Inn of the Sixth Happiness (1958)
Twentieth Century Fox
Producer Buddy Adler
Director Mark Robson
Music played by Royal Philharmonic Orchestra/Malcolm Arnold

Notes (i) The film score won Malcolm Arnold an Ivor Novello award, presented by the Songwriters Guild of Great Britain in 1959.

(ii) Music from the film was arranged for brass band by Edrich Siebert (1961), and for orchestra by Christopher Palmer (1992) (also transcribed for symphonic wind) – see Appendix B.

Article Alan Poulton, 'The 'Inn' Plaque' in North Wales – *Beckus* 112, Spring 2019

The Boy and the Bridge (1959)
Xanadu Productions
Producers David Eady and Kevin McClory
Director Kevin McClory
Music played by Orchestra/Malcolm Arnold
Notes The Overture from the film was arranged for orchestra, probably by Tony Fones (c.1959) – see Appendix B.

Solomon and Sheba (1959) [part/uncredited]
Edward Small Productions for United Artists
Producer Ted Richmond
Director King Vidor
Music played by Orchestra/Franco Ferrara
Notes Though Mario Nascimbene is credited with the entire score, Malcolm Arnold was brought in by the producer in to write 3 cues, totalling around 3 mins 45 secs.

Suddenly Last Summer (1959) [part]
Columbia Pictures/Horizon
Producer Sam Speigel
Director Joseph L Mankiewicz
Music played by Orchestra/Buxton Orr
Notes Arnold was taken ill during the composition of the soundtrack, having completed only about one-fifth in full score. However, he did leave a number of sketches of various 'themes' and 'characters' from which Buxton Orr was able to complete the score.

The Angry Silence (1960)
Beaver Films
Producers Richard Attenborough and Bryan Forbes
Director Guy Green
Music played by Orchestra/Malcolm Arnold

Tunes of Glory (1960)
Knightsbridge Films
Producer Colin Lesslie
Director Ronald Neame
Music played by Orchestra/Malcolm Arnold

The Pure Hell of St Trinian's (1960)
Hallmark/Tudor/Vale Productions
Producers Frank Launder and Sidney Gilliat

Director Frank Launder
Music played by Orchestra/Malcolm Arnold

No Love for Johnnie (1960)
Five Star Films
Producer Betty E Box
Director Ralph Thomas
Music played by Orchestra/Malcolm Arnold
Notes Music from the film was arranged as a concert suite by Philip Lane – see Appendix B.

Whistle Down the Wind (1961)
Allied Film Makers/Beaver Films
Producer Richard Attenborough
Music played by Orchestra/Malcolm Arnold
Notes Music from the film was arranged as a suite for small orchestra by Christopher Palmer
  (1991) – see Appendix B.

On the Fiddle (1961)
Coronado Productions
US title Operation Snafu (Situation Normal – All Fouled Up)
US Alt title Operation War Head
Producer Benjamin Fisz
Director Cyril Frankel
Music played by Orchestra/Malcolm Arnold

The Inspector (1962)
Red Lion Films
US title Lisa
US Alt title Lisa and the Police Inspector
Producer Mark Robson
Director Philip Dunne
Music played by Orchestra/Malcolm Arnold

The Lion (1962)
Samuel G Engel Productions for Twentieth Century Fox
Producer Samuel G Engel
Director Jack Cardiff
Music played by Orchestra/Malcolm Arnold

Nine Hours to Rama (1962)
Red Lion for Twentieth Century Fox
US Alt title Nine Hours to Live
Producer/Director Mark Robson
Music played by Orchestra/Malcolm Arnold

Tamahine (1963)
Seven Arts for Associated British Picture Corporation
UK Alt title The Natives are Restless Tonight

Producer John Bryan
Director Phillp Leacock
Music played by Orchestra/Malcolm Arnold
Notes Music from the film 'Royal Fireworks Music' for wind band – see Appendix B.

The Chalk Garden (1963)
Quota Rentals/Ross Hunter Productions
Producer Ross Hunter
Director Ronald Neame
Music played by Orchestra/Malcolm Arnold

The Thin Red Line (1964)
A.C.E. Films/Security Productions
Producers Philip Jordan and Sidney Harmon
Director Andrew Marton
Music played by Orchestra/Malcolm Arnold

The Heroes of Telemark (1965)
Benton Film Productions
Alt title The Unknown Battle
Producer Benjamin Fisz
Director Anthony Mann
Music played by Orchestra/Malcolm Arnold
Notes Music from the film was was arranged as a suite for orchestra by John Gibbons (2017) – see Appendix B.

Sky West and Crooked (1966)
John Mills Productions
UK Alt title Bats with Baby Faces
US title Gypsy Girl
Producer Jack Hanbury
Director John Mills
Music played by Orchestra/Malcolm Arnold

The Great St Trinian's Train Robbery (1966)
Braywild
Producer Leslie Gilliat
Directors Frank Launder and Sidney Gilliat
Music played by Orchestra/Malcolm Arnold

Africa: Texas Style (1966)
Vantors/Ivan Tors Films
US title Cowboy in Africa
Producers Andrew Marton and John Pellatt
Director Andrew Marton
Music played by Orchestra/Malcolm Arnold

The Reckoning (1969)
Columbia Pictures Corporation
UK *Alt title* A Matter of Honour
Producer Ronald Shedlo
Director Jack Gold
Music played by Orchestra/Malcolm Arnold

The Battle of Britain (1969) [uncredited]
Spitfire Productions for United Artists (1969)
Producers Harry Saltzman and Benjamin Fisz
Director Guy Hamilton
Music played by Orchestra/Malcolm Arnold and William Walton (for the March)
Notes Arnold assisted in the orchestration of several sections and was responsible for re-scoring and expanding Walton's original soundtrack. However, after it had been recorded, the score was rejected and Ron Goodwin was asked to write a new score. Lawrence Olivier threatened to remove his name from the film if some of Walton's music was not reinstated, so they used Walton for the 'Battle of the Air' sequence and Ron Goodwin for the rest. The latest DVD allows you to choose from the Goodwin or Walton scores (although there is some question about whether the Walton score has been synchronised with the film correctly).
Articles
(i) Günther Kögebehn, 'The Battle of Britain: a film score Odyssey' – *Beckus* 54, Autumn 2004
(ii) James Brooks Kuykendall, 'Battle of Britain: New evidence in the autograph manuscripts' – *Beckus* 114, Autumn 2019
(iii) Alan Poulton, 'Battle of Britain: letters from Walton' – *Beckus* 114, Autumn 2019

David Copperfield (1969)
Omnibus Productions
Producer Frederick Brogger
Director Delbert Mann
Music played by Orchestra/Malcolm Arnold
Notes Music from the film was arranged as a suite for orchestra by Philip Lane (1999)– see Appendix B.
Article Alan Poulton, '1969: A busy year for Malcolm' – *Beckus* 114, Autumn 2019

The Wildcats of St Trinian's (1980) [part]
Wildcat Film Productions
Producer E M Smedley-Aston
Director Frank Launder
Music played by Orchestra/Frank Barber
Notes The film uses some of the original music which Malcolm Arnold had composed for earlier St Trinian's films [1. School song 2. The Charge of the Fourth Form 3. End Titles 4. St Trinian's March]; the rest of the soundtrack was written by James Kenelm Clarke.

Appendix D. List of documentaries

See also 'The Arnold Documentaries' (*Maestro* 6).

Avalanche Patrol (1947)
Universal Pictures (USA) for the Swiss Avalanche Patrol
Alt title Swiss Avalanche Patrol
Director Jack Swain
Music played by London Symphony Orchestra/John Hollingsworth
Article Alan Poulton, 'Avalanche Patrol' – *Beckus* 100, Spring 2016

Accident Prevention Concerns You (1948)
A series of nine flashes ('shorts')
Crown Film Unit for the Royal Air Force
Music played by London Symphony Orchestra/John Hollingsworth

Charting the Seas (1948)
Realist Film Unit for the Central Office of Information/Admiralty
Director Harold Lowenstein
Music played by London Symphony Orchestra/John Hollingsworth

Gates of Power (1948)
Anglo-Scottish Films for the Central Office of Information/Board of Trade/GFD
Alt title Stairway to the Sea
Director Anthony Squire
Music played by London Symphony Orchestra/John Hollingsworth

Report on Steel (1948)
Data Film Productions for the Central Office of Information/Ministry of Supply
Director and Editor Michael Orrom
Music played by London Symphony Orchestra/John Hollingsworth
Notes In 1951 Arnold re-worked the music into his Symphonic Study 'Machines' for brass, percussion and strings Op.30 (q.v.).

Mining Review (series) (1948)
Data Film Unit for the Central Office of Information and the National Coal Board
Director Michael Orrom
Music played by Orchestra/Malcolm Arnold
Notes We have not been able to ascertain whether Malcolm Arnold provided the title music for this long-running series, which ran from 1947 to the demise of the National Coal Board Film Unit in 1984 (after 420 editions), or whether he provided the soundtrack only to the

1948 series of monthly programmes. At its height the series was watched by 12 million people and distributed to over 700 cinemas nationwide, mostly in mining areas. The series producer was Donald Alexander.

Every Drop to Drink (1948)
World Wide Pictures for Metropolitan Water Board/ British Lion
Alt title Hydrography
Director Mary Francis
Music played by London Symphony Orchestra/John Hollingsworth

Queen o' the Border (1948)
Crown Film Unit for the Central Office of Information/Board of Trade/Hawick Hosiery Manufacturers Association
Alt title Hawick Weaving
Director Martin Wilson
Music played by London Symphony Orchestra/John Hollingsworth

Women in Our Time (1948)
'This Modern Age' series No.22
This was the first of many films in the `This Modern Age' series for which Arnold provided the music; it is probable that Muir Mathieson conducted the London Symphony Orchestra in them all. The series producer for the J Arthur Rank Organisation was Sergei Nolbandov and the series associate producer and Literary Editor was James L Hodson.

Lancashire's Time for Adventure (1948)
'This Modern Age' series No.23
Alt title Cotton

The Struggle for Oil (1949)
'This Modern Age' series No.25
Music played by London Symphony Orchestra/Muir Mathieson

European Volunteer Workers (EVWs) (1949)
Data Film Unit for the Central Office of Information/Ministry of Labour
Alt title Code Name: Westward Ho!
Director Mary Beales
Music played by London Symphony Orchestra/John Hollingsworth

This Farming Business (1949)
Greenpark Productions for the Central Office of Information
Music played by London Symphony Orchestra/John Hollingsworth

The Frasers of Cabot Cove (1949)
Greenpark Productions for the Central Office of Information/Commonwealth Relations Office
Alt title An Island Story
Director Humphrey Swingler
Music played by London Symphony Orchestra/John Hollingsworth

Drums for a Holiday (1949)
Anglo-Scottish Films/British Lion for Cadbury and the Gold Coast Cocoa Bean Industry
Director A R Taylor
Music played by Orchestra/James Walker

Magic Electrons: Terra Incognita (1949)
Verity Films
Music played by Orchestra/Malcolm Arnold

The Fair County of Ayr (1949)
Anglo-Scottish Films/British Lion
Alt title The Beautiful County of Ayr
Director Charles Heath
Music played by Philharmonia Orchestra/James Walker
Notes Some of the music was later incorporated into the second movement of the Four
    Scottish Dances Op.59
Articles Alan Poulton, 'The Fair County of Ayr' – *Beckus* 109, Summer 2018

Dollars and Sense (1949)
Crown Film Unit for the Central Office of Information and the Economic Information Unit
Director Diana Pine
Music played by London Symphony Orchestra/John Hollingsworth

Fight for a Fuller Life (1949)
'This Modern Age' series No.30

Trieste: Problem City (1949)
'This Modern Age' series No.32

When you went away (1949)
'This Modern Age' series No.33

The Riddle of Japan (1949)
'This Modern Age' series No.35

Where Britain Stands (1950)
'This Modern Age' series No.36

Science in the Orchestra (1950)
A series of three film 'shorts'
[1. Hearing the Orchestra 2. Exploring the Instruments 3. Looking at Sounds]
Realist Film Unit for the Central Office of Information/Ministry of Education
Director Alex Strasser
Music played by London Symphony Orchestra/Muir Mathieson

'Oil Review' series: No.5 (1950)
Greenpark Productions

Music played by London Symphony Orchestra/John Hollingsworth
Notes A total of eighteen 'Oil Reviews' were issued between 1950 and 1953

Ideas at Work (1950)
Crown Film Unit for the Economic Co-operation Administration (USA)
Alt title ECA Productivity Team

Fifty Acres (1950)
Greenpark Productions for the British Electrical Development Association (1950)
Director Peter Plaskitt
Music played by Orchestra/John Hollingsworth

Airways (series Nos. 1-3) (1950)
[1. Standard Beam Approach 2. Airport Control 3. Area Control]
John Marvel Productions
Music played by London Symphony Orchestra/John Hollingsworth

This is Britain (series) (1950)
Crown Film Unit/Merlin Films for the Central Office of Information/Board of Trade
Music played by London Symphony Orchestra/John Hollingsworth
Notes A series of documentaries about Britain in the 1940s and 1950s for which Arnold may
well have provided the title music – the series producer was Michael Hankinson.

Alien Orders (1950)
*Crown Film Unit for the Central Office of Information/Foreign Office and Commonwealth
Relations Office*
Alt title Malaya
Music played by London Symphony Orchestra/John Hollingsworth

Power for All (1950)
'The Changing Face of Europe' series No.1
Wessex Film Productions for the Economic Co-Operation Administration (USA)
Directors Anthony Squire and Graham Wallace
Music played by Orchestra/Malcolm Arnold
Notes The six-part series had an alternative title 'Grand Design Progress Report from
Europe' – the Series Producer was Ian Dalrymple.

Men and Machines (1950)
'The Changing Face of Europe' series No.4
Wessex Films for the Economic Co-Operation Administration
Alt title Industry
Director Diana Pine
Music played by Orchestra/Malcolm Arnold

Farming Review No.1 (1950)
Greenpark Productions/Film Producer's Guild for Harry Ferguson
Director Joe Mendoza

Articles Joe Mendoza, 'Me and Malcolm Arnold' – *Beckus* 37, Summer 2000 & *Maestro* 1, October 2014, in which he recalls Arnold's 'March of the Little Tin Tractors'.

Antony and Cleopatra (1951)
Parthian Productions/Young America Films
Music played by Philharmonia Orchestra/Malcolm Arnold

Julius Caesar (1951)
Parthian Productions/Young America Films
Music played by Philharmonia Orchestra/Malcolm Arnold
Notes The above two drama-documentaries were adapted (condensed) from the original plays and were aimed at high school students in America as a supplement to a study of Shakespearean plays in both theatre and drama classes.

Local Newspaper (1952)
Crown Film Unit for Central Office of Information/ Foreign, Commonwealth Relations and Colonial Offices
Music played by London Symphony Orchestra/John Hollingsworth

Channel Islands (1952)
British Transport Films for British Transport Commission
Director Michael Orrom
Music played by Orchestra/Malcolm Arnold

The Island (1952)
Data Film Productions for the Anglo-Iranian Oil Company
Alt title Kent Oil Refinery
Directors and commentary writers Peter Pickering and John Ingram
Music played by London Symphony Orchestra/John Hollingsworth

Copenhagen, City of Towers (1952)
Seven League Productions (Loew's Incorporated/MGM) for Fitzpatrick Traveltalk
Director Hans M Nieter
Notes Music of various composers arranged by Malcolm Arnold.

Warm Welcome (1952)
Greenpark Productions for Anglo-Iranian Oil Company/Film Producers Guild
Director Joe Mendoza
Producer Humphrey Swingler
Notes According to Joe Mendoza, Malcolm Arnold provided the soundtrack to this documentary.

Man of Africa (1953)
Group Three/British Lion
Original title Soil Erosion
Alt title Kigezi Story

Appendix D. List of documentaries

Director Cyril Frankel
Music played by Orchestra/Malcolm Arnold

Powered Flight: the Story of the Century (1953)
Shell Film Unit for Shell Petroleum and the Royal Aeronautical Society
Director Stuart Legg
Music played by Orchestra/Malcolm Arnold

Major Farming (1953)
Verity Films/Film Producers Guild for the Ford Motor Company
Director Joe Mendoza
Notes We have not been able to verify that Malcolm Arnold was the composer of the soundtrack.

Royal Tour – New Zealand (1954)
'The Royal Tour' series No.3
Pathé Documentary Unit for Associated British Pathé
Series producer Howard Thomas
Music played by Orchestra/Muir Mathieson

Welcome the Queen! (1954)
Pathé Documentary Unit for Associated British Pathé
Producer Howard Thomas
Music played by Orchestra/Muir Mathieson
Notes Written in conjunction with Sir Arthur Bliss who composed the title music, the March 'Welcome the Queen!'

War in the Air
See main catalogue

Let Go For'ard! (1955)
Esso Film Unit for Esso Petroleum
Director Geoffrey Gurrin
Music played by Orchestra/Malcolm Arnold

Roses Tattoo (1956)
Anglo-Scottish Pictures for Cadbury
Music played by Orchestra/James Walker
Notes Not be confused with the contemporaneous feature film 'The Rose Tattoo' starring Burt Lancaster and Anna Magnani with music by Alex North.
It is probable that the correct title for this documentary is in fact 'Roses All the Way', an advertisement for Cadbury's chocolate and produced by Anglo-Scottish Pictures. The latter had been responsible, along with Malcolm Arnold who wrote the music and James Walker who was the conductor, for providing the soundtrack to another Cadbury film in 1949 'Drums for a Holiday' (q.v.).

Coupe des Alpes (1958)
Shell Film Unit for Shell Petroleum
Director John Armstrong
Music played by Orchestra/Malcolm Arnold

North Sea Strike (1968)
Gerald Holdsworth Productions for the Esso Petroleum Company
Director Don Kelly
Music played by Orchestra/Malcolm Arnold

Divertimento (1968)
Verity Films/Film Producers Guild for the British Petroleum Company
Alt title Oil under the Microscope
Director David Cons
Series producer Seafield Head
Notes Filming oil through a microscope and other optical devices, the weird and colourful world revealed is set to the music of Arnold's Divertimento for flute, oboe and clarinet Op.37 (q.v.).

NEL Offshore News (1975)
National Engineering Laboratory for the Central Office of Information/Department of Industry
Series producer Howard Thomas
Director K R Offord
Notes Frank Chacksfield composed part of the soundtrack

Appendix E. Arrangements of music by other composers

Three short pieces arranged for solo clarinet (c.1938)
[1. Pardon me pretty baby 2. Georgia 3. I ain't got nobody]

Reginald King: 'Song of Paradise' arranged for trumpet solo and small orchestra (1940)
First performance Malcolm Arnold (Tpt.)/John Moravia and his orchestra – Pier Head Pavilion, Llandudno, 25 March (Easter Sunday) 1940
Article Alan Poulton, 'Arnold plays King in Llandudno' – *Beckus* 96, Spring 2015

'Silver Threads among the Gold' arranged for trumpet and piano (1941)
First performance Malcolm Arnold – Royal College of Music, June 1941 (Student Concert)

Two Pieces arranged for trumpet, horn and trombone (1943)
[1. Motet: Marie Assumptio 2. Machaut: Double Hoquet]
First performance Malcolm Arnold (Tpt.), Dennis Brain (Hn.), George Maxted (Tbn.) – St Peter's Church, Eaton Square, London, 15 August 1943
First broadcast performance [No.2 only] Members of the BBC Symphony Orchestra/Constant Lambert – Third Programme, 1 February 1949
Article William C. Lynch 'Brothers in Brass: the friendship of Malcolm Arnold and Dennis Brain' – *Maestro* 2, October 2015

Indian National Anthem: orchestration (1947)
Commissioned by the Indian High Commissioner, Krishna Menon
Notes See Paul Jackson, 'The Brilliant and the Dark', Ashgate, 2003, p.30

Albeniz: Tango in D from 'Espana' Op.165 No.2 arranged for orchestra (1953)
Instrumentation 2/2/2/2 – 4/2/3/0 – timp. perc. hp. str.
First broadcast performance BBC Concert Orchestra/Rae Jenkins – Light Programme, 12 December 1959
Publisher Good Music, 2003

Two Purcell songs arranged for contralto and string orchestra (1959)
1.'On the brow of Richmond Hill' – Words: Tom Durfey
  2.'Mad Bess' or 'Bess of Bedlam' – Words: Anon]
Written for Pamela Bowden

Duration 6'
First performance Pamela Bowden/Richmond Community Centre String Orchestra/Malcolm
   Arnold – Richmond Community Centre Hall, Surrey, 26 March 1959
Publisher Novello (No.1 only)
Notes The score to No.2 is lost

Christmas Carols arranged for guitar, baritone, SATB chorus, brass band and orchestra (1960)

Written for a charity matinee in aid of the 'Save the Children Fund'
[1. The First Nowell 2. Away in a Manger 3. Good King Wenceslas]
Instrumentation (max.) 2/2/2/2 – 4/2/3/1 – timp. perc.(2) pno. cel. hp. str.
First performance Regimental Band of the Coldstream Guards/Theatre Royal Orchestra/
   Malcolm Arnold – Drury Lane Theatre, London, 19 December 1960

Thomas Merritt: Coronation March arranged for brass band (1967)

Score dated St Merryn, Cornwall, 17 December 1967
Duration 5'
First performance St Dennis Silver Band/St Agnes Silver Band/Malcolm Arnold – Truro
   Cathedral, 16 March 1968
Publisher Henrees Music, 1968; Studio Music
Notes (i) Composed in 1901 to celebrate the Coronation of King Edward VII
Article Alan Poulton, 'Thomas Merritt' (with music example) – Maestro 4, October 2017

Thomas Merritt: Anthems and Carols arranged for SATB chorus, brass bands and orchestra (1968)

[1. Carol: 'Awake with Joy, Salute the Morn' 2. Carol: 'Send out The Light' 3. Anthem: 'The
   Eyes of all wait for Thee' 4. Anthem: 'Awake up my glory']
Score dated St Merryn, Cornwall, 12-17 January 1968
Instrumentation (max.) 2+picc./2/2/2 – 4/3/3/1 – timp. perc.(3) hp. str.
First performance Mixed choirs/Penzance Orchestral Society/Cornwall Symphony
   Orchestra/St Agnes Silver Band/St Dennis Silver Band/Malcolm Arnold – Truro Cathedral
   16 March 1968
First broadcast performance (No.4) above performance – Radio 3, 17 April 1968
Notes The March was performed by the University of Salford Brass Band on 20 November
   1991 as part of the Arnold 70th Birthday celebrations
Article Alan Poulton 'Thomas Merritt' (with music example) – Maestro 4, October 2017

Walton: String Quartet: arrangement of fourth movement for string orchestra (1971)

First performance Academy of St Martin-in-the-Fields/Neville Marriner – Australia, 2 March
   1972 (Perth Festival)
Publisher OUP, 1973 (as 'Sonata for String Orchestra')

Appendix F. Other major articles in *Beckus* and *Maestro* (1991–2020)

'Beckus' is the quarterly newsletter and 'Maestro' is the annual journal of the Malcolm Arnold Society; see www.malcolmarnoldsociety.co.uk.

Adni, Isaac: 'Malcolm Arnold's Concertos: masterpieces of mélange' – *Maestro* 5, October 2018

Ainsley, Rob: 'The Symphonies', from Classic CD, July 1994 – *Beckus* 13, July 1994; *Maestro* 1, October 2014

Amis, John: 'Not Malcolm the Dandipratt but Malcolm the Trumpeter' – *Beckus* 17, Summer 1995; *Maestro* 1, October 2014

Angel, David: 'Sir Malcolm Arnold's String Quartets' – *Beckus* 54, Autumn 2004; *Maestro* 5, October 2018

Anon: 'Artist and Composer', from Music Magazine, May 1964 – *Beckus* 20, Spring 1996; *Maestro* 1, October 2014

Anon: 'Arnold and all that Jazz', from Classic CD Review (1993) – *Beckus* 10, October 1993

Anon: 'ISM Distinguished Musician Award' – *Beckus* 58, Autumn 2005; *Maestro* 6, October 2019

Anon: 'The Malcolm Arnold Trumpet Competition' – *Beckus* 88, Spring 2013

Anon: 'Music from the Films' – a discussion between Muir Mathieson and Malcolm Arnold, (recorded 21 May 1954) – *Beckus* 97, Summer 2015

Baggs, Geoffrey: 'Malcolm Arnold at Home', from the Western Morning News, 17 October 1969 – *Beckus* 92, Spring 2014

Budd, Vincent: 'Malcolm Arnold and John Lord' (in three parts) – *Beckus* 26, Autumn 1997; *Beckus* 27, Winter 1997; *Beckus* 28, Spring 1998; *Maestro* 1, October 2014

Burton-Page, Piers: 'Toward the Unknown Region' (review) – *Beckus* 56, Spring 2005; *Maestro* 6, October 2019

Burton-Page, Piers: 'Ken Jones Portrait' – *Beckus* 70, Autumn 2008; *Maestro* 6, October 2019

Burton-Page, Piers: 'In Memoriam Richard Hickox' – *Beckus* 72, Spring 2009

Burton-Page, Piers: 'Malcolm Arnold: an Individual Voice' – *Beckus* 96, Spring 2015

Burton-Page, Piers: 'The Odyssey of Malcolm Arnold' – *Maestro* 2, October 2015

Burton-Page, Piers; 'Hunt the Chaconne' – *Beckus* 101, Summer 2016

Burton-Page, Piers: 'Watching the flames together' (Malcolm Arnold and Ralph Vaughan Williams) – *Beckus* 103, Winter 2016

Burton-Page, Piers: 'The Arnold Quartets revisited' – *Maestro* 5, October 2018

Burton-Page, Piers: '2020 and 2021: Beethoven and Arnold' – *Beckus* 116, Spring 2020

Burton-Page, Piers: 'Malcolm Arnold and Julian Bream' – *Maestro* 7, October 2020

Butterworth, Arthur: 'An Ebullient Young Man' – *Beckus* 48, Spring 2003; *Maestro* 4, October 2017

Catterick, Tony: 'Charles 'Charlie' Gregory' – *Beckus* 110, Autumn 2018
Clark, Edward: 'A day with Sir Malcolm Arnold' – *Beckus* 49, Summer 2003; *Maestro* 4, October 2017
Clark, Edward: 'Sir Malcolm Arnold and Russia' – *Beckus* 68, Spring 2008
Cleary, Tony: 'Sir Malcolm Arnold – Patron and Friend' – *Beckus* 57, Summer 2005
Cole, Hugo: 'Malcolm Arnold at 60', from Music & Musicians, October 1981 – *Beckus* 97, Summer 2015
Craggs, Stewart; 'A bibliographical update' – *Maestro* 3, October 2016
Craggs, Stewart: 'Letters between Sir Malcolm Arnold and Sir William Walton' – *Maestro* 4, October 2017
Cushion, Terry: 'Arnold films on DVD', *Beckus* 99, Winter 2015
Cushion, Terry: 'Statue of Malcolm Arnold unveiled' – *Beckus* 106, Autumn 2017
Cushion, Terry: 'Malcolm Arnold Discography' – *Maestro* 7 Supplement, October 2020
Davis, Andrew: 'Why I am a member of the Society' – *Beckus* 35, Winter 1999; *Maestro* 1, October 2014
Dunstan, David: 'The Symphonies on record' – *Beckus* 76, Spring 2010
Dunstan, David: 'The choral music: CD required' – *Beckus* 118, Autumn 2020
East, Robert: 'Arnold sings praise of the West Country', from the Western Morning News, 20 October 1992 – *Beckus* 7, January 1993; *Maestro* 1, October 2014
Ellerby, Martin: 'Tributes' and 'Malcolm Arnold Variations' – *Beckus* 113, Summer 2019
Ellin, Benjamin: 'A Conductor's View' – *Beckus* 70, Autumn 2008
Ellis, David: 'Working with Malcolm Arnold' – *Beckus* 63, Winter 2006; *Maestro* 6, October 2019
Finch, Hilary: 'Cheers for Arnold', from The Times, 6 September 1994 – *Beckus* 14, October 1994
Graham-Jones, Ian: 'Some memories of Malcolm Arnold in Cornwall' – *Beckus* 91, Winter 2013
Graham-Jones, Ian: 'Malcolm Arnold and Thomas Merritt' – *Beckus* 103, Winter 2016
Green, Andrew: Book Review: 'The Life and Music of Sir Malcolm Arnold by Piers Burton-Page', in Classical Music Magazine – *Beckus* 16, Spring 1995; *Maestro* 1, October 2014
Gregory, Colin: 'Padstow pays Tribute', from the Western Morning News, 3 June 2014 – *Beckus* 94, Autumn 2014
Gwynn, Lucy: 'Exhibition at Eton College' – *Beckus* 106, Autumn 2017
Harley, Mike: 'Birmingham Royal Ballet' – *Beckus* 102, Autumn 2016
Harris, Adrian; 'The Eton Arnold project' – *Beckus* 101, Summer 2016
Harris, Paul: 'Devils, Donkeys and Dinosaurs' (Gordon Jacob) – *Beckus* 74, Autumn 2009; *Beckus* 102, Autumn 2016; *Maestro* 7, October 2020
Hayes, Emma: 'Arnold in Cornwall' – *Beckus* 37, Summer 2000; *Maestro* 1, October 2014
Hibbert, Stan: 'Malcolm Arnold: The Repertoire Guide', from Classical Music, 2 December 1995 – *Beckus* 19, Winter 1995
Hibbert, Stan: 'Arnold Celebrations 96: some reflections' – *Beckus* 24, Spring 1997, *Maestro* 1, October 2014
Hibbert, Stan: 'The Arnold Awards' – *Beckus* 27, Winter 1997; *Maestro* 1, October 2014
Hibbert, Stan: 'Conferment Day at the RNCM' – *Beckus* 28, Spring 1998; *Maestro* 1, October 2014
Hilton, Janet; 'Playing Malcolm's clarinet works' – *Beckus* 101, Summer 2016
Houston, Dan: 'Back in Watford', from Classic CD Review, (1992) – *Beckus* 5, April 1992

Hunt, Philip: 'Malcolm Arnold in Cornwall' – *Beckus* 59, Winter 2005; *Maestro* 6, October 2019

Huntley, John: 'Something Special' – *Beckus* 33, Summer 1999; *Maestro* 1, October 2014

Huss, Fabian: 'Malcolm Arnold's chamber music' – *Beckus* 101, Summer 2016

Iannucci, Armando: '…reflects on the death of Malcolm Arnold', from *Gramophone*, November 2006 – *Beckus* 111, Winter 2018

Jackson, Paul: 'The name game' – *Beckus* 37, Summer 2000; *Maestro* 1. October 2014

Jackson, Paul: 'Lost and Found' – *Beckus* 21, Summer 1996; *Maestro* 1, October 2014

Jameson, Michael: 'The Conductor Remembered' – *Beckus* 93, Summer 2014

Jenkins, Lyndon: 'Tunes Foremost' from Classical Music Magazine, 11 February 1984 – *Beckus* 44, Spring 2002; *Maestro* 3, October 2016

Kehoe, John: 'On and Off the Record' – *Beckus* 95, Winter 2014

Keight, Lennie: 'Malcolm Arnold at the Proms' – *Beckus* 78. Autumn 2010

Kögebehn, Günther: 'A Grand Grand Event' (Moyland Castle) – *Beckus* 50, Autumn 2003

Kögebehn, Günther: 'Malcolm Arnold: a composer of real music' (book review) – *Beckus* 70, Autumn 2008; *Maestro* 6, October 2019

Kögebehn, Günther: 'An Arnold evening on BBC4' ('Our Classical Century' series) – *Beckus* 113, Summer 2019

L.S.: 'The Huddersfield Interview' – *Beckus* 22, Autumn 1996; *Maestro* 1, October 2014

Lancaster, Julian: 'The British Academy of Composers and Songwriters Fellowship' from 'The Works', Autumn 2001 – *Beckus* 43, Winter 2001; *Maestro* 3, October 2016

Lane, Philip: 'Reconstructing Arnold's film scores' – *Beckus* 100, Spring 2016

Lebrecht, Norman: [entry in] 'The Companion to 20th-Century Music' (*Publisher* Simon and Schuster, 1992) – *Beckus* 9, July 1993; *Maestro* 1, October 2014

Lebrecht, Norman: 'Malcolm and Malcolm: your time will come', from the Daily Telegraph, 25 July 2001 – *Beckus* 42, Autumn 2001

Llewellyn, Keith and Brand, Frank: 'The Malcolm Arnold Bronze' – *Beckus* 69, Summer 2008; *Maestro* 6, October 2019

Long, Barry Arnold: 'Mon Uncle', *Beckus* 17, Summer 1995: *Maestro* 1, October 2014

Lynch, Irene Duffy: 'A Truly Great Man' – *Beckus* 56, Spring 2005

Lynch, William C: 'Brothers in Brass: the friendship of Malcolm Arnold and Dennis Brain' – *Maestro* 2, October 2015

McCann, Donal: 'Arnold at Eton' – *Beckus* 107, Winter 2017

Mellor, David: 'What about Arnold?', from The Spectator, 7 December 1991 – *Beckus* 3, January 1992

Mellor, David and Matthew-Walker, Robert: 'The significance of Malcolm Arnold', a session recorded at the 2018 Malcolm Arnold Festival – *Beckus* 112, Spring 2019

Meredith, Anthony: 'The Persuasive Pamela' (Pamela Watson) – *Beckus* 77, Summer 2010; *Maestro* 7, October 2019

Meredith, Anthony: 'The Royal Ballet' – *Beckus* 86, Autumn 2012

Meredith, Anthony; 'New kid on the block' (in three parts) – Part 1: A talent to amuse – *Beckus* 103, Winter 2016; Part 2. A hill to climb – *Beckus* 104, Spring 2017; Part 3. A talent to confuse – *Beckus* 105, Summer 2017

Meredith, Anthony: 'Pilot Officer Philip Arnold (1919-1940)' – *Maestro* 5, October 2018

Meredith, Anthony: 'The Auction in Retrospect' – *Beckus* 111, Winter 2018

Meredith, Anthony: 'Lot 86: a lot of mixed memories' – *Beckus* 112, Spring 2019

Meredith, Anthony: 'A Catalogue of Achievement' – *Maestro* 6, October 2019

Mitchell, Donald: 'Cradles of the New' (three essays from the book – published David Higham) – *Maestro* 4, October 2017

Newman, Archie: '70th birthday reception – Press Release, 27 May 1992' – *Beckus* 5, July 1992; *Maestro* 1, October 2014

Newman, Bill: 'A Grand Grand Composer' (interview) – *Beckus* 46, Autumn 2002; *Maestro* 4, October 2017

Pearn, John: 'An encourager of young musicians' – *Beckus* 118, Autumn 2020

Penny, Andrew: 'In Interview' (with Jeremy Siepmann) from 'Naxos: Maestro's Musings', 23 September 2010 – *Beckus* 119, Winter 2020

Petri, Michala: 'Working with Malcolm Arnold' – *Maestro* 7, October 2020

Pfaff, Philip: 'A Friendly Word' – *Beckus* 18, Autumn 1995; *Maestro* 1, October 2014

Pfaff, Philip: 'The making of a musician' – *Beckus* 80, Spring 2011

Porter, Andrew: 'Homage to the Queen', from 'Musical Events', February 1954 – *Beckus* 79, Winter 2010

Poulton, Alan: 'The Hunt for Purple Dust' – *Beckus* 47, Winter 2002

Poulton, Alan: 'The Arnold documentaries: an update' (in two parts) – *Beckus* 50, Autumn 2003; *Beckus* 52, Spring 2004

Poulton, Alan: 'John Kuchmy – a man of many parts' – *Beckus* 96, Spring 2015

Poulton, Alan: 'The BBC Genome Project' – *Beckus* 97, Summer 2015

Poulton, Alan: 'Arnold by Arrangement' – *Beckus* 98, Autumn 2015

Poulton, Alan: 'The Birmingham International Wind Competition, 1966' – *Maestro* 2, October 2015

Poulton, Alan: 'The National Youth Orchestra and Malcolm Arnold' – *Maestro* 2, October 2015

Poulton, Alan: 'The Arnold Bournemouth Connection' (in two parts) – Part 1: 1947-1956, *Beckus* 99, Winter 2015; Part 2: 1970 to date – *Beckus* 101, Summer 2016

Poulton, Alan: 'Malcolm Arnold and Ruth Gipps' – *Beckus* 100, Spring 2016

Poulton, Alan: '150 Symphony Performances' – *Beckus* 100, Spring 2016

Poulton, Alan: 'Works for soloist and strings' – *Beckus* 101, Summer 2016

Poulton, Alan: 'Jacob-Arnold connections' – *Beckus* 102, Autumn 2016

Poulton, Alan: 'Arnold's published film music' – *Maestro* 2, October 2016

Poulton, Alan: 'The Haweses: a musical family' – *Maestro* 2, October 2016

Poulton, Alan: 'Leicestershire Schools Symphony Orchestra' – *Beckus* 106, Autumn 2017

Poulton, Alan: 'Thomas Merritt' – *Maestro* 4, October 2017

Poulton, Alan: 'Arnold's 'other' ballets' – *Maestro* 4, October 2017

Poulton, Alan: 'Arnold's film and concert music on 7" vinyl' – *Maestro* 4, October 2017

Poulton, Alan: 'The search for the missing scores' Part 1 – *Beckus* 107, Winter 2017; Part 2 – *Beckus* 116, Spring 2020

Poulton, Alan: 'Arnold the conductor' – *Beckus* 110, Autumn 2018

Poulton, Alan: 'Lamond Clelland: piccolo player' – *Maestro* 5, October 2018

Poulton, Alan: 'Arnold and the BBC' – *Maestro* 5, October 2018

Poulton, Alan: 'Reel Streets' (Arnold film locations survey) Part 1 – *Beckus* 113, Summer 2019; Part 2 – *Beckus* 114, Autumn 2019

Poulton, Alan: 'Judith Bailey and Malcolm Arnold' – *Beckus* 114, Autumn 2019

Poulton, Alan and David Dunstan: 'The other Malcolm Arnold' – *Beckus* 114, Autumn 2019

Poulton, Alan: 'Arnold on the small screen' – *Maestro* 6, October 2019

Poulton, Alan: 'Arnold's feature films and their literary sources' – *Maestro* 6, October 2019

Poulton, Alan: 'The Arnold documentaries' – *Maestro* 6, October 2019

Poulton, Alan: 'The Accordion Concerto that never was' – *Beckus* 115, Winter 2019

Poulton, Alan: 'The Trianon Enigma' – *Beckus* 117, Summer 2020

Poulton, Alan: 'The film music: looking for Vol.3' – *Beckus* 118, Autumn 2020

Poulton, Alan: 'Feature films in performance' – *Maestro* 7, October 2020

Poulton, Alan: 'A Cornish Diary' – *Maestro* 7, October 2020

Pullen, Penny: 'Christmas at Craigmore' – *Beckus* 31, Winter 1998; *Maestro* 1, October 2014

Reilly, Robert: 'English Enigma' (in two parts) – *Beckus* 33, Summer 1999; *Beckus* 35, Winter 99; *Maestro* 1, October 2014

Richmond, Neil: 'Transcribing Arnold's works' – *Beckus* 108, Spring 2018

Searle, Humphrey: 'Malcolm Arnold: a birthday tribute', from a BBC broadcast, October 1971 – *Beckus* 105, Summer 2017

Shaw, Richard; 'Investigating Sir Malcolm Arnold's Songs and Arias' – *Beckus* 48, Spring 2003; *Maestro* 4, October 2017

Smith, Adrian, 'The Music of Malcolm Arnold' – *Beckus* 19, Winter 1995; *Maestro* 1, October 2014

Smith, Graham: 'Alf Arnold: the black sheep of the family?' – *Beckus* 99, Winter 2015

Smurthwaite, Alan: 'Sheila Arnold' – *Beckus* 74, Autumn 2009; *Maestro* 7, October 2020

Stasiak, Christopher: 'The Symphonies of Malcolm Arnold', from 'Tempo' (CUP, 1987) – *Maestro* 4, October 2017

Stevens, Rebecca: 'Malcolm Arnold' (in five parts) – *Beckus* 81, Summer 2011; *Beckus* 82, Autumn 2011; *Beckus* 83, Winter 2011; *Beckus* 84, Spring 2012; *Beckus* 86, Autumn 2012

Thöne, Raphael: 'Elgar's influence on Malcolm Arnold' – *Maestro* 5, October 2018

Towell, Philip: 'Memories of Sir Malcolm' – *Beckus* 22, Autumn 1996; *Maestro* 1, October 2014

Wadeson, Barry, 'Philip Pfaff', from the Northampton & District Organists' Association Newsletter, 2009 – *Beckus* 94, Autumn 2014

Webber, Michael: 'The First Malcolm Arnold Festival' – *Beckus* 38, August 2000

Whittle, David: 'Malcolm Arnold and Bruce Montgomery' – *Beckus* 109, Summer 2018

Wood, Philip: 'Malcolm Arnold, the English Shostakovich' – *Beckus* 3, January 1992; *Maestro* 1, October 2014

Wood, Philip: 'Composer of the Week: 17-21 October 1994' – *Beckus* 15, Winter 1994; *Maestro* 1, October 2014

Wood, Philip and Paul Serotsky: 'Book Review: The Pimlico Dictionary of Twentieth Century Composers' – *Beckus* 34, Autumn 1999; *Beckus* 36, Spring 2000; *Maestro* 1, October 2014

Wood, Philip: 'The First Arnold Festival:2000' – *Beckus* 39, Winter 2000; *Maestro* 3, October 2016

Wood, Philip: 'The Brilliant and the Dark' (book review) – *Beckus* 48, Spring 2003; *Maestro* 4, October 2017

Index of works

Divertimento (1968) 114
Divertimento (Duo) for two B flat clarinets Op.135 (1988) 81
Divertimento for wind trio Op.37 (1952) 24
Divertimento No.1 for orchestra Op.1 (1942) 8
Divertimento No.2 for orchestra Op.24 (1950) 17
Divertimento No.2 for orchestra Op.75 (1961) 50
Dollars and Sense (1949) 110
Dream City for piano (1938) 2
Drums for a Holiday (1949) 110
Dunkirk (1957) 103
Duo for flute and viola Op.10 (1945) 11
Duo for two cellos Op.85 (1965) 56

Eight Children's Piano Pieces Op.36 (1952) 23
Electra: incidental music (1955) 33
Elektra: Ballet in one act Op.79 (1963) 52
Elektra: Ballet Suite Op.79a (2004) 53
English Dances for orchestra (Set 1) Op.27 (1950) 18
English Dances for orchestra (Set 2) Op.33 (1951) 21
Espionage: ATV series (1963) 53
European Volunteer Workers (EVWs) (1949) 109
Every Drop to Drink (1948) 109

Fanfare for a Festival, for brass and percussion (1955) 33
Fanfare for a Royal Occasion (1956) 36
Fanfare for Louis for two trumpets (or two cornets) (1970) 67
Fanfare for one, eighty years young: for solo trumpet (1971) 69
Fanfare for the Farnham Festival (1961) 49
Fanfare for three trumpets (1949) 16
Fanfare for three trumpets (no date) 85
Fantasy for audience and orchestra Op.106 (1970) 68
Fantasy for bassoon Op.86 (1965) 56
Fantasy for bass trombone and piano (1950) 17
Fantasy for brass band Op.114a (1973) 71
Fantasy for cello Op.130 (1987) 80
Fantasy for clarinet Op.87 (1966) 56
Fantasy for descant recorder Op.127 (1986) 78
Fantasy for double bass (no date) 85
Fantasy for flute and guitar (1960) 47
Fantasy for flute Op.89 (1966) 57
Fantasy for guitar Op.107 (1970) 68
Fantasy for harp Op.117 (1975) 73
Fantasy for horn Op.88 (1966) 57
Fantasy for oboe Op.90 (1966) 57
Fantasy for trombone Op.101 (1969) 65
Fantasy for trumpet Op.100 (1969) 65
Fantasy for tuba Op.102 (1969) 65

It Started in Paradise (1952) 98

John Clare Cantata for chorus and string orchestra Op.52a (2015) 34
John Clare Cantata for SATB chorus and piano duet Op.52 (1955) 34
Jolly Old Friar, for unison voices and piano (1965) 59
Journey: Ballet (1979) 30
Julius Caesar (1951) 112

'Katherine, Walking and Running' for two violins (1952) 26
Kensington Gardens: song cycle for medium voice and piano (1938) 3
Kingston Fanfare for brass (1959) 44

Lancashire's Time for Adventure (1948) 109
Larch Trees: Tone poem for orchestra Op.3 (1943) 8
Leonora No.4 (Beethoven-Strasser) Overture for large orchestra (1961) 51
Let Go For'ard! (1955) 113
Little Suite No.1 for brass band Op.80 (1963) 53
Little Suite No.1 for orchestra Op.53 (1955) 34
Little Suite No.2 for brass band Op.93 (1967) 60
Little Suite No.2 for orchestra Op.78 (1962) 52
Little Suite No.3 for brass band Op.131 (1987) 80
Little Suite No.4 for orchestra Op.80a (1999) 54
Little Suite No.5 for orchestra Op.93a (2000) 60
Local Newspaper (1952) 112

Magic Electrons: Terra Incognita (1949) 110
Major Farming (1953) 113
Man of Africa (1953) 112
March: 'Overseas' for military band Op.70 (1960) 47
MA Serenade: Ballet (2014) 18
Men and Machines (1950) 111
Mining Review (series) (1948) 108
'Morning Moon' for solo piano (1944) 11
Music for a Pageant: composite work (1948) 14
Music for You: signature tune for BBC Television series (1958) 43

NEL Offshore News (1975) 114
Nine Hours to Rama (1962) 105
No Highway (1950) 97
No Love for Johnnie (1960) 94, 105
North Sea Strike (1968) 114

Oboe Quartet Op.61 (1957) 41
'Oil Review' series: No.5 (1950) 110
On the Fiddle (1961) 105
Overture [Suite] for wind octet arranged by the composer for piano duet (1940) 5

Index of works

The Shipwright's Song: for unison voices (1966) 59
The Sleeping Tiger (1954) 100
The Smoke: Overture for orchestra Op.21 (1948) 15
The Song of Accounting Periods for high voice and piano Op.103 (1969) 65
The Sound Barrier (1952) 98
The Sound Barrier: Rhapsody for orchestra Op.38 (1952) 24
The Story of Gilbert and Sullivan (1953) [arranger/uncredited] 99
The Struggle for Oil (1949) 109
The Tempest (1954) 28
The Thin Red Line (1964) 106
The Three Musketeers (2006) 88
The Three Musketeers: Ballet [sketches] (1975) 74
The Turtle Drum: a children's play for television Op.92 (1967) 59
The Wildcats of St Trinian's (1980) [part] 107
The Woman for Joe (1955) 101
This Christmas Night for unaccompanied SATB chorus (1967) 63
This Farming Business (1949) 109
This is Britain (series) (1950) 111
Thomas Merritt: Anthems and Carols arranged for SATB chorus, brass bands and orchestra
    (1968) 116
Thomas Merritt: Coronation March arranged for brass band (1967) 116
Three Fantasies: Ballet (1995) 79
Three Fantasies for piano Op.129 (1986) 79
Three Piano Pieces (1937) 2
Three Piano Pieces (1943) 8
Three Shanties for Wind Quintet Op.4 (1943) 9
Three short pieces arranged for solo clarinet (c.1938) 115
Tiger in the Smoke (1956) 102
Tommy's Titifala: song for unison voices (c.1966) 59
To Youth: Suite for orchestra (1948) 15
Toy Symphony Op.62 (1957) 41
Trapeze (1956) 92, 102
Trevelyan: Suite for ten instruments Op.96 (1967) 62
Trieste: Problem City (1949) 110
Trio for flute, trumpet and cello (c. 1940) 6
Trio for flute, viola and bassoon Op.6 (1943) 10
Tunes of Glory (1960) 104
Two Bagatelles for piano Op.18 (1947) 14
Two Canons for piano solo (c.1937) 2
Two Ceremonial Psalms for unaccompanied SSA boys' chorus Op.35 (1952) 22
Two John Donne Songs for tenor and piano Op.114b (1974) 71
Two Part Songs (1939) 3
Two Piano Pieces (1941) 7
Two Pieces arranged for trumpet, horn and trombone (1943) 115
Two Purcell songs arranged for contralto and string orchestra (1959) 115
Two Sketches for oboe and piano (1941) 6
Two Songs for voice and full orchestra [sketches] (1988-89) 82

Index of works

Index of people

Index of people

Index of people

Index of people

Index of people

General index

General index

Printed in Great Britain
by Amazon

27215509R00089